COT DEATHS

Coping with Sudden
Infant Death Syndrome

Jacquelynn Luben

Bedford Square Press

Published by
BEDFORD SQUARE PRESS of the
National Council for Voluntary Organisations
26 Bedford Square, London WC1B 3HU

First published by Thorsons 1986
Revised edition published by Bedford Square Press 1989

Typeset by BookEns, Saffron Walden, Essex
Printed and bound in Great Britain at
The Camelot Press plc, Southampton

British Library Cataloguing in Publication Data
Luben, Jacquelynn
   Cot deaths: coping with sudden infant death
   syndrome. – 2nd ed. – (Survival handbooks).
   1. Babies. Sudden infant death syndrome. Personal
   adjustment of parents
   I. Title   II. Series
   306.8'8

ISBN 0-7199-1264-4

This book is is dedicated to my mother, Sadie Beaver, who has faced all the problems that life has aimed at her with unshakeable optimism, and to my daughter, Amanda, whose short stay in my life changed its direction.

Acknowledgements

I should like to express my gratitude to the parents who allowed me to interview them and to record their experiences, and to the 'professionals', all of whom gave generously of their time and furnished me with useful information, which has been most helpful in the writing of this book. I should particularly like to mention Dr John Grabinar, General Practitioner, since I have quoted at length from conversations with him.

I should also like to thank Lady Limerick and Mrs Reed of the Foundation for the Study of Infant Deaths, for taking the time to read and comment on this book, and Lady Limerick for her Foreword.

Contents

Foreword

The sudden and unexpected death of a baby for no obvious
reason is one of the most harrowing and haunting tragedies that
can afflict a family: parental shock and bewilderment can be
devastating and long lasting as agonizing fears and unfounded
guilt feelings arise. It is also one of the most distressing and
baffling tragedies with which officials, health professionals and
relatives are involved.

Each year in Britain, about 2,000 babies between the ages of
one week and two years die suddenly and unexpectedly, 90 per
cent before the age of eight months. In about 1,500 of these cot
deaths no adequate reason for the death is found at the post-
mortem examination and these are described as Sudden Infant
Death Syndrome. Although a rare tragedy affecting one baby in
every 500 live births, cot death is the most common kind of
death in babies after the first month of life.

Jacquelynn Luben describes in considerable detail her own
experience, reactions and feelings and those of some other
parents who suffered similar tragedies. She has also consulted
the views of individual doctors and nurses and the Foundation
for the Study of Infant Deaths, and has put forward sensible
suggestions on how officials and health professionals can ease
the trauma of a cot death tragedy.

Jacquelynn Luben describes parents' reactions immediately
following the discovery of their dead child and how to cope
with the coroner's investigation and other procedures; the
support needed from health professionals, relatives and other
befrienders, and the vulnerability of newly bereaved parents.
She mentions some of the practical steps to take which may
help parents to face up to the death and the importance of
recognizing the grief and needs of older children. Jacquelynn

Luben assesses the value of talking with other parents and becoming involved in activities to support research as a constructive way of paying tribute to the child that has died. She also considers the emotional and practical problems associated with a subsequent pregnancy and caring for the next child, and ends by reflecting on how she refound happiness and what has been achieved in public understanding in the years since her own baby's death.

Jacquelynn Luben's baby died in 1971, the same year that the Foundation for the Study of Infant Deaths was founded following a symposium held in April 1970 in Cambridge attended by doctors and parents to collate information on the problem.

Since 1971 the Foundation has raised funds and sponsored over 120 medical research projects into cot deaths, conducted by paediatricians, physiologists, physicists and nurses in hospitals, the community and universities. Some projects are examining the physiological development of babies, variations in the heart rate, the development of stable breathing patterns, the influence of respiratory infections and different sleep states. Slowly but surely research is filling important gaps in the knowledge of heart and lung physiology in the vulnerable period of life between one and eight months (when most sudden infant deaths occur), with a view to determining whether all infants are at risk of sudden death by virtue of age or only those with an inherent or acquired vulnerability.

Other research has been examining the characteristics of babies who die unexpectedly and has been able to identify some infants at increased risk and study the possibilities for prevention.

Another research project has been evaluating different ways of supporting cot death families with their subsequent baby by comparing the home use of apnoea monitors with detailed monitoring of weight gain, using the specially designed Sheffield centile weight charts.

The Foundation has given support to more than 9,000 bereaved families and has striven to improve public understanding of the nature and scale of the problem and to encourage tactful management in order to lessen any distress arising from the coroner's investigation and to enhance the quality of explanation and support given by health care professionals and by parent befrienders.

The Foundation gives personal support to bereaved families by letter, telephone and leaflets and offers to put parents in touch with formerly bereaved parents, Friends of the

Foundation, who offer an individual befriending service. The Foundation also gives advice and information to parents who are expecting a subsequent child.

The Foundation also acts as a centre of information about cot deaths for parents and professionals. It publishes a series of leaflets to help parents at the time of bereavement and when caring for a subsequent child, and newsletters describing the research findings. It also has videos for training professionals and officials about the impact on the family of a sudden infant death and suggestions of appropriate ways of giving support.

Many officials and professionals may be involved with cot death – ambulance staff, Accident and Emergency Departments, police, coroners and their officers, general practitioners, pathologists, paediatricians, health visitors, midwives, social workers, funeral directors, mortuary attendants, registrars of death and ministers of religion.

It is hoped that this book will be of practical use to people in any of these professions by making them aware of reactions of parents, and that it will bring comfort and reassurance to many parents who are bereaved in this baffling way to read of how others coped with similar problems.

SYLVIA LIMERICK
Vice-Chairwoman
The Foundation for the Study of Infant Deaths

Introduction

When my first child was born, I was told the following story: a young inexperienced mother kept creeping up to her baby to see if it was breathing. Her husband teased her for being so nervous, but one day she discovered him placing a mirror to the baby's lips and realized that he was as insecure as she was. At that time, I was amused, because my baby snored noisily, and I envisaged no occasion when I should need to be reassured that he was still breathing.

I did not know, however, that there was a situation in which a baby would pass from life to death totally without warning. So ignorant was I that, four years later when faced with that situation, I still knew nothing of the condition known as 'cot death' or Sudden Infant Death Syndrome.

When I was first asked to write this book, my instinct was to refuse, though, since the death of my baby daughter, I had learned a great deal more about the subject. By this time, I had described my experience in detail, in an as yet unpublished autobiographical book, I had written articles on cot death, both before and after my second daughter was born, as well as many letters to other bereaved mothers, and I felt I had said everything I could say. In addition, so much time had passed since baby Amanda's death that it seemed arrogant and presumptuous of me to think I could write about the emotions I felt so long ago. I was also doubtful whether I, a non-professional, was the right person to tackle this sort of book.

However, after considerable thought, I began to wonder if my lack of 'expertise' might not be an advantage. I, at least, might be able to write a book for laymen – by a layman – a book without the jargon that the professionals sometimes accidently include; a book that would try to deal with some of the trivial questions and problems that the 'experts' do not necessarily consider. I began to think that even my detachment might be of benefit, for I could now put forward not only my own viewpoint, but that of other bereaved parents in a more objective way than would have been possible previously.

I regard this book as a description of a journey towards recovery, and I have tried to show what happens, from the beginning of that 'journey' – the tragedy itself – through various stages, from disbelief to acceptance, from passivity to a desire to do something positive, until the time comes when life has, to a certain extent, resumed its original pattern.

I have been asked why I have included so much detail of the first days after the death of the baby, when there is little likelihood of bereaved parents having acquired this book at that early stage. Of course, if parents or other relatives do obtain this book within the first day or so, I would like to think it will give them some practical help. However, parents who read the book some time after the tragedy may still wish to compare how they were treated or how they felt with the experiences of other people, and in addition, health professionals may also gain some insight into the needs of newly-bereaved parents and so perhaps be able to give them the understanding and help they need.

However much knowledge is dispensed, there is very little that can be of help to us when the discovery of the sudden death of our baby is made. I do believe, however, that parents need all the information they can get, to help them cope with the weeks and months after the death of their baby. Any traumatic experience such as this sets people apart, and the more knowledge that is spread in the community, enabling both the bereaved and others to understand and to talk about the situation, the less isolated they will be.

Here, then, is the book I, myself, might have wanted to buy when baby Amanda died in 1971. It does not purport to replace good friends, comforting relatives or organizations like the Foundation for the Study of Infant Deaths and its associated local groups. However, I hope that on those occasions when bereaved parents feel totally alone, it may lessen their feelings of isolation just a little.

What do I mean by cot death?

During this book, I shall be using the term 'cot death' to describe the natural death of an apparently healthy baby – a sudden and unexpected event not foreseen by either its parents or the medical profession. This will also include those deaths not adequately explained by the post-mortem examination, which are often registered as Sudden Infant Death Syndrome.

Sometimes, an explanation for the death is found at the post-mortem examination. The baby may be shown to have had a virus, for example, not recognized by those people who saw the baby before its death. This may still be regarded as a cot death.

How has the term 'cot death' been used by others?

The term 'cot death' was first used in the 1950s to cover the sudden and unexpected death of an apparently healthy baby in its sleeping accommodation.* At that time, the term *included* baby deaths where a cause, such as unsuspected congenital abnormality, rare metabolic disease or an overwhelming infection or injury, was later identified by the post-mortem examination; a very few may have been found to be cases of infanticide.

In the mid-60s customary use of the term was narrowed to cover only those cases in which the information available (including the post-mortem examination) did not reveal an adequate cause or causes of death and this was synonymous with the term 'SIDS' (Sudden Infant Death Syndrome) which was defined first in the USA in 1969 as 'the sudden death of any infant or young child which is unexpected by history and in which a thorough post-mortem examination fails to demonstrate an adequate cause of death.'

A certain amount of confusion has arisen during the last fifteen years or so, since some people, including members of both the medical profession and the media, are still using the term 'cot death' to describe any unexpected infant death, whilst others are using it to describe only those deaths for which there is no adequate explanation at the post-mortem examination.

Parents whose babies have died from natural, although little-understood causes, are very distressed when the term 'cot death' is used to include cases of suspected infanticide. In addition, periodically, dramatic reports have appeared in the media alleging that a large proportion of cot deaths are not

* In the USA, the term 'crib death' is used instead of 'cot death'.

natural deaths, but are deliberately caused by the parents of the baby. It is important to note that a study of the deaths from all causes of nearly one thousand babies, commissioned by the DHSS, which announced its findings in January 1985, showed that only nine cases were officially recorded as infanticide and only a further fifteen aroused doubts or unproven suspicions – a maximum of 2.5 per cent. It should be made absolutely clear that when it is proved that parents have deliberately caused their babies' deaths, these cases are not included in statistics on cot deaths.

At the other end of the spectrum, where a post-mortem examination reveals a severe infection and the cause of death is given as, for example, viral pneumonia, parents sometimes feel guilty that they failed to recognize their baby's illness. However, research has shown that babies may succumb to severe disease, before signs of illness are obvious. Sometimes, a term such as 'viral pneumonia' is mentioned on the death certificate, even though it may not, in the pathologist's view, wholly explain the cause of the baby's death.

In any case, all parents whose babies have died unexpectedly, even if an explanation or partial explanation is found at the post-mortem examination, deserve support and explanation, and such parents might still find much of the information contained in this book helpful and appropriate.

As the techniques of paediatric pathologists become more sophisticated, it is possible that more unsuspected infections, abnormalities or diseases will be revealed. However, the parents informed of such findings will be no more or less shocked and grief-stricken than those who have no other verdict than that their child died of 'cot death' or SIDS.

1 A tragedy occurs

What is it like to experience a cot death?

If you are a parent trying to recover from that unforgettable
experience, then you will need no descriptions, but there are
variations from one case to another as the following examples
show.

In my own case, which occurred some years ago, my
daughter, who was seven-and-a-half weeks old, was put to bed
at around nine o'clock after a long feed. She had been very
playful that evening and my husband and I had taken great
delight in seeing her kicking and smiling. However, she always
cried at being put in her cot and that night was no exception. I
had been accustomed to leaving her to cry for a little while and
usually she soon dozed off to sleep. The cry was usually a
complaining, grizzling sound and, had it changed character and
become a cry of genuine discomfort, I believe I would have
recognized the difference. Thus, when my husband and I went
to bed ourselves about two hours later, we assumed she was
asleep, but went over to the cot just the same, to check that all
was well. She was unusually high up in the cot, squashed into
the corner, and it was this strange position that made me feel ill
at ease. As a result, we bent to hear her breathing, but heard no
sound at all. We moved an arm and found it was quite limp and
then, finally we turned on the light in the room and saw at last
the white face that confirmed our gradually increasing fears.

Jane and David lost their nine-week-old baby, Naomi, in
autumn 1981. It was one o'clock in the morning when they
found her, having put her in the carry cot after a feed at 8 p.m.
They had been out to their friends' house, taking advantage of
the mobility of a baby of that age, and had checked her a
couple of times during the evening. It was a cold and windy

night, so that when they brought her from their friends' house to the car, they kept the bedclothes around her, their main concern being to keep her warm and not wake her at that stage. Only when they arrived home and stripped off the extra blankets did they realize that something was wrong.

On a Sunday afternoon in December, Maureen A. and her husband Rod found their nine-and-a-half week old son, Timothy, dead. They did not call an ambulance, as they lived quite close to the local hospital, but made their way quickly to the casualty department by car. Maureen rushed into the hospital with the baby in her arms, and on hearing that the baby was not breathing, the staff bypassed the reception procedures, took the baby from her and installed her in a side room accompanied by a member of staff. She and her husband were not left alone, and eventually the baby's death was confirmed by the hospital paediatrician.

On the May night that Sue and Neville's seven-week-old baby son, Anthony, died, it was Neville who discovered him, when he went to wake him for his 10 p.m. feed. Living in a close-knit rural community in Suffolk, they were on first-name terms with the local doctors, one of whom Sue immediately rang, and he arrived within five minutes.

Maureen B. found her five-week-old baby, Michelle, in the morning at around 8 o'clock. She had glanced in the baby's room to check her a couple of times, but assumed that Michelle was still sleeping, since she had slept through the night on some occasions previously. Maureen was on her own at the time, except for her two small boys, as her husband, Tony, was away. When she discovered the baby, her screams attracted the attention of her neighbours, who came to assist her. One, a nurse, tried mouth-to-mouth resuscitation and an ambulance was called.

Lynne and Paul's baby, Andrew, was also found in the morning. He had woken up and cried in the middle of the night, but Lynne had not gone to him; sometimes he would cry but settle down again. They did not hear any more from him and assumed that he had managed to sleep through the night without a feed, since he had done so once before. Paul found the baby; he called Lynne and she rushed in. She rang 999 since it was obvious that they could do nothing, and called in a neighbouring doctor. They followed the ambulance to the hospital and were told immediately they arrived that the baby was dead.

In Sylvia Limerick's Survey of the Management of Unexpected Infant Deaths, which is included in *Sudden Infant*

Deaths: Patterns, Puzzles and Problems by Jean Golding, Sylvia Limerick and Aidan Macfarlane (Open Books Publishing Ltd, 1985), she mentions a very small percentage of doctors who were not prepared to attend at the house when summoned to a dead baby. In practice, from the point of view of speed, it is probably best in urban areas or where distances are not great, to call an ambulance first and the doctor in addition. If there is any possibility of resuscitation, the ambulance staff will be trained to carry it out.

Dr G. told me that he very often advises people when summoned to a patient who has 'collapsed' (that is, possibly the patient is dead, but the relatives are unsure), ' "Phone for an ambulance and I'll be along." That way it saves time. If they get the ambulance service, the ambulance will arrive at more or less the same time as we do.' In such circumstances, it is possibly comforting to have the doctor present as well as the ambulance, since he may be a familiar figure to the family.

I asked Dr C. what he would do if called to a suspected cot death. He told me that if he was able to certify death, he would have to inform the Coroner.

If there was any doubt as to whether or not the baby was, in fact, dead, the doctor would attempt mouth-to-mouth and nose resuscitation, try to keep the heartbeat going, get an ambulance and get the baby to the nearest paediatric unit quickly.

If a baby was actually declared dead at home, he or she would most probably be transported to the mortuary. If there was a possibility of the baby still being alive, it would be taken to hospital; however a doctor in that situation might well refrain from stating categorically that the baby was dead, in order that it could be taken quickly from the home.

The immediate reaction of parents to the discovery of their babies is often one of numbness. Many are capable of quite coolly taking the necessary steps of calling the ambulance and/ or the doctor and sometimes attempting some form of resuscitation. I remember carrying out these tasks as if in a dream. I found it difficult to believe that such a thing could possibly happen to our family and some illogical part of me believed that something was going to happen to put everything magically right. And since the ambulance man tried artificial respiration throughout the journey to hospital, I suppose that I still hoped that the colour would come back into my baby's cheeks and she would start breathing again. Of course, on arrival at the hospital, her death was confirmed, and in spite of the feeling of disbelief, it was not in any way a real surprise to me.

Other parents felt the same way. On the one hand, they were in no doubt, from the strange and awkward positions in which they found their respective babies or from the sight of the babies' faces, that they were dead, but at some other level they felt that some miraculous happening would change everything. At this stage parents felt they needed to be told in a direct way that their baby was dead.

Maureen and Rod had been given that information and, in addition, had been told that the death was likely to have been a cot death, but that there would have to be a post-mortem.

In Sue and Neville's case, the doctor confirmed immediately that the baby was dead and said that he thought that the baby had inhaled vomit. (This was very much a standard diagnosis at that time when the term 'cot death' was not so widely used.) The doctor told Sue and Neville that he was obliged by law to inform the police. He also telephoned the undertaker, who called shortly afterwards to take away the baby's body. Later, the doctor returned to bring drugs for Sue. Sue and Neville felt that their treatment at this stage was very much due to their close association with doctors, nurses and police in the small village in which they lived.

Jane and David, however, who were not invited to go with the ambulance, did not receive the essential confirmation of their baby's death until the following day. Jane was aware that the ambulance men were not treating Naomi like a live baby, but she still felt in need of a definite statement making the situation quite clear.

They wrapped her up and took her out and I saw the way she was wrapped. He'd taken the blanket off the carry cot and *bundled* her in it. Not wrapped her in it as you would a baby you were trying to keep warm.
But because you don't have to deal with death, you can look at a corpse and still refuse to accept that they're dead.

Jane would have preferred to have been told by the ambulance men that her baby was dead. However, they are not medically qualified to give out this information. What was surely unforgivable was that Jane and David were not subsequently immediately informed of the baby's death, and that they had to seek this information themselves.

David had to ring the hospital the next day. They didn't contact us. I think they assumed that we knew she was dead, but you don't [know]. You need someone to tell you coldly and bluntly. You knew she was dead, you knew it was all over, but then . . . at the back of your mind, you had vague hopes – that they'd got her to the hospital and they'd managed to resuscitate her and that nobody was telling you.

I, too, remember listening to the nurse in Casualty where my daughter, Amanda, was taken by ambulance, saying: 'You know what I'm going to tell you, don't you?' and thinking 'Is she telling me that the baby is dead, or is she telling me that they have revived her, but because of lack of oxygen, she is brain-damaged?' Of course, the nurse then went on to speak in such a way that it became obvious that my baby had died. After asking various questions, I was escorted home by the ambulance men who had brought me and the baby to hospital, my husband, Michael, having remained at home with our young son.

Saying goodbye

It is difficult to remember now whether I was offered the opportunity of seeing and holding Amanda again before leaving the hospital, and difficult too to know what my reply was or would have been. The climate has changed since that time, and there is now a great emphasis on the importance of parents being able to say both 'hello' and 'goodbye' to babies who have died within a few hours of birth. The parents of a baby who has died when a few weeks or months old are not in the same situation, for the baby's existence has definitely been acknowledged in a way that the stillborn baby may not have been. The feelings of the latter parents invited to see and hold their dead baby may be exactly the same as if they were asked if they wished to see any loved member of their family after death.

Some people may feel a revulsion at the prospect of seeing the corpse and may prefer to remember the loved one in their living state, whilst others may be fearful at the idea of seeing any deterioration. Some parents might like to have a last look at the baby, without picking him up. I think that the doctor or nurse on duty should give the parents these choices, giving them a warning of the state the baby is likely to be in, but without prejudicing them, one way or another.

On balance, my own feeling is that I think I would like to have been invited to say goodbye to my daughter, but I am glad that when I last held her, she was still soft and warm. I do not think I would have gained comfort from finding her body stiff and cold, though that grim experience may be the necessary confirmation of death to some parents.

Lynne and Paul were asked by a nurse at the hospital if they would like to see their baby again, and they were taken to the

chapel at the hospital. They were glad to be given this opportunity, although they did not hold the baby, who was covered
up. (Lynne had, however, held the baby at home before the
arrival of the ambulance.) Lynne could only see his face, but
she wished that they had washed him before she had been
taken to him, as his nose was running. Small things become
important to bereaved parents.

Maureen and Rod were taken to see their baby again after
speaking to the hospital paediatrician. Rod was upset by the
experience, but Maureen would have liked to have stayed
longer.

They took us through an unmarked door to what was obviously a sort
of chapel. They had actually got him laid out on a high bed. We
thought he would be in a cubicle somewhere in Casualty or in a side
room. There were flowers, and it was not what we had expected. What
I did find disturbing was that his face was visible but the rest of him
was covered by this long white sheet, and he'd got a high frilly collar.
When the doctor asked if we wanted to see him again, she asked a
nurse to 'clean him up a bit', which at the time I thought was not the
happiest choice of words. I don't know whether they'd tried inserting a
tube through his windpipe. I was disturbed at the sight of this high
frilly collar because I thought it must be there to hide something. I felt
that I was not intended to pick him up, so I didn't.

The situation that Maureen described was likely to have
occurred as a result of tracheotomy, that is, a tube being
inserted into the baby's windpipe in order to introduce air to
the lungs. This form of artificial respiration is likely to have
been carried out in this instance, since the baby was taken
directly to hospital and no previous attempt at resuscitation had
been made by any medical person.

Jane felt she would have liked to have gone to hospital with
the ambulance and to have been able to have that short time
with Naomi, to sit and hold her. However, Jane was in an
emotional state at the time. She says: 'What I really needed was
the ambulance men to calm me down and say, "Now, I think it
would be best that you come with us and see the doctors at the
hospital." When it is your first experience of death, you need to
be guided.'

Maureen B. did not go with the ambulance and she too
regretted that in retrospect. She had not held the baby after
discovering her, and therefore, she did not feel she had really
said goodbye to her daughter.

Dr G. confirmed that he would encourage parents to
accompany the baby – or any child – to hospital. 'Parents should

be satisfied that everything possible has been done; though it may be that there is nothing to be done. It helps parents to come to terms with the death if they feel they've done all they can, including being present and available should the doctors want them.' Dr G. also felt strongly that, in general, the family should always be invited to see and/or touch a dead person, adult or child, after the death had been confirmed. Most doctors, he felt, should realize that this emotional need should be satisfied. In addition, surviving children might be deeply affected and it could well help them to accept the situation, if they are able to see their brother or sister one last time.

However, the fear that the baby is not in a state to be seen or picked up is not necessarily voiced by the bereaved parents at the time of death. This makes it imperative that hospital authorities or doctors in attendance take the initiative in offering them this facility (but not bullying them into it), for in their vulnerable and shocked state, the parents may not be capable of expressing their wishes, or may be fearful of having to fight hospital procedures.

If the parents have seen and held the baby immediately after the discovery of the death, then seeing the baby again at the hospital may be less of a traumatic experience than if they did not see the dead baby before (if, for example, only one parent went into the room when the baby was discovered).

The prospect of facing the transformation of the baby from life to death is a daunting one and if the parents (or other children) cannot face this vision, I do not feel that it should be forced upon them even though someone may think that it would be 'good for them' to see the dead baby. I remember that as a thirteen-year-old, when my grandmother died, I was worried that I would be asked to go into her room and see her, and I was very relieved at not being asked.

In any case, some parents wish to retain the memory of a live child, and that wish should be respected. Sue did not see her baby after Neville had found him dead, and did not feel that she had missed out in any way.

I still have no regrets about not seeing him, because I put to bed a very fit, very noisy baby. We'd had a lovely day together – the four of us – digging an allotment. I brought the two children home, bathed them and gave them their tea and put them to bed; and that was my last memory of him. I never wanted to see him. I had no wish to see him and I have no regrets whatsoever.

Sometimes at the hospital parents will be asked questions, partly in order to complete records, and partly to assist in revealing the cause of the baby's death. Parents may find these enquiries rather harrowing, but when they are finally left alone, they enter into a no man's land where the territory is unfamiliar and they have no idea of their destination. If the baby is discovered in the morning, a number of things may take place during the day. If the baby is found during the night, the procedures may not begin until the next day. In my own case, it was midnight when the ambulance brought me home, but I was incapable of sleeping. I felt directionless. I didn't know what we had to do next, and sleeping seemed to be part of an old routine that was no longer applicable.

Similarly, Jane and David were left in this limbo in the middle of the night. 'One minute you're a happy little family with a baby and then you find your baby dead and, in the space of an hour, it's all over.' Jane and David were additionally neglected in the first hours after death because it happened at a weekend and during their GP's holiday, when an unknown locum deputized for him. This caused problems for Jane, who was not offered any medication to suppress lactation, though she was offered sedatives.

Sedatives and tranquillizers

I asked Dr G. what he thought about the prescribing of sedatives at this stage. He was reluctant to offer sedatives to the mother unless she was in such a distraught state that she could not think or talk clearly, which was very rare.

Sometimes it is suggested that when someone gets upset or tearful, the doctor should give something, and I say, 'What do I have to give? I can't make the dead person come to life again. That is what she wants and I can't give it.' If she wants to cry, that isn't a disease, that's normal.

Dr C. felt that his decision would be based on the knowledge of the parents. He commented that he would try to avoid using a sedative if possible (though he might offer one for sleep purposes) but certainly would not offer a tranquillizer. 'It would depend very much on the parents and the support the mother and father had from each other and the rest of the family.'

Maureen B.'s doctor left her a prescription for tranquillizers but she did not use them, and similarly, Jane was offered them and refused them.

I didn't want to be put to sleep. If I'd had tranquillizers then, I would have had more and I would have blotted it out; those first ten days were *so* bad, that it could only get better, and at least you could see that. (It's not this sort of Never-Never-Land of floating in between.)

Maureen A. was given an envelope containing four sleeping pills by the paediatrician, which were later exchanged for slightly stronger ones from her GP. She took them on the first two nights after the death and on the night before the funeral. She did not take them during the day, but was glad of the help to get off to sleep on those particular nights.

Lynne's doctor did not recommend having tranquillizers; he told her to try and manage without them. She did, however, take sedatives for a couple of weeks to help her sleep, though she did not always succeed in getting a full night's sleep. She was in agreement with her doctor, and would not have wanted to take tranquillizers.

I asked Mrs J., a hospital nurse, for her opinion on tranquillizers or sedatives. She felt that whether the parents would want them or not would depend on their temperament. Many people would not want to take tranquillizers, but those who did should not be condemned. I asked her if she felt parents should be offered such drugs/medication as a matter of course.

I think the doctor *should* offer them. Some people are helped by them; and in particular, sleeping pills can help a bit. If you go to bed, and night after night you can't sleep, and there are other children, you're not going to be able to help them at all. Also, if a mother is very distraught – for a few days or a few weeks – it might help.

My own feelings were the same as Jane's. I was not offered tranquillizers and I had no regrets about that. Initially, at any rate, one is almost anaesthetized by shock and I had the feeling of being in a dream. Instinctively, I felt that I had to face up to the reality without being dulled in any way. Had I taken tranquillizers or sedatives, I would have simply been warding off the day when I would have to face reality. I think it would have been much worse to have had the pain temporarily blotted out by tranquillizers, because I would then have had to face it again when my mind was clear. It seemed to me better to face that pain at its most intense, and to know that as it receded, there was a genuine improvement, even though this improvement, if measured against the whole amount of the sorrow, was just a tiny fraction day by day.

Nevertheless, I have to say that I have always been a good sleeper, and if I had had difficulties with sleep which I could not resolve, I might have felt differently about sleeping pills at

least. However, I do remember waking up on the night after
Amanda's death, at around the time when she would have
wanted her feed. I found it very ironic that I had awoken
spontaneously, with my mind clear, when on previous nights,
when she had woken me, I was sleeping soundly and was
reluctant to be disturbed.

Sue took both sleeping tablets and tranquillizers. On the first
night, she was given two tablets and told to take them with a
hot drink, following by a further two if they did not work. The
four tablets sent Sue off to sleep for eight hours. After that she
was given two varieties of tablets and told to take one sort
during the day, and the other to enable her to sleep at night. I
asked her if she found them helpful and I found her answer
ambivalent.

They probably were – I very much regret having had so many – it got
me through the first week up until the funeral. After that I gave up the
sleeping tablets. But it took me a long, long time to come off the
tranquillizers – a long, long time. I regret the ease with which I was
given more tranquillizers afterwards. I only had to say to the doctor
that I'd had a bad two days and my prescription was immediately
renewed and upped.

I got the impression that Neville believed more strongly than
Sue in the benefit of the tranquillizers and sleeping pills, and I
wondered if he found it so difficult to bear his wife's grief that
he was relieved to see it subdued.

It is so often much more a part of a woman's nature to cry
than a man's, that possibly men wish to stem the tears. (Women
during their pregnancy and in the first few months after
childbirth are, in any case, likely to be more tearful than usual
because of hormonal changes.) At the same time, there may be
an assumption by the husband that his wife is weaker than he
and less able to bear the pain without some form of medication.
I think this is a false assumption, once again inspired by the
more expressive and emotional nature of women. Women,
perhaps more than men, need to let their feelings out, and tears
are a very natural expression of the grief they obviously feel.

I am not suggesting that a mother should not be given
tranquillizers, or more particularly sleeping tablets, if she really
wants them. However, I think it is a mistake for them to be
prescribed automatically at this stage, instead of allowing the
mother to express her grief. With hindsight, Sue felt she would
have benefited from more counselling, or from being able to
talk to someone who had had the same experience.

At this very early stage, it is important that husband and wife are able to express their grief to each other; that the local GP is able to provide support, both by seeing the bereaved parents himself, and by ensuring that his staff, in the form of the Health Visitor or District Midwife are calling in to see the parents, and that close friends and relations do their best to see the couple, to share their grief and to allow them to talk of their experience, if they wish to. Tranquillizers are a poor substitute for this support, and have the added disadvantage of being potentially addictive, as demonstrated in recent studies.

One mother commented to me that one does take an aspirin to relieve a headache. This is true, but generally, when one takes pain-killing medication to solve a short-term pain, the reason for the pain is likely to disappear during the same period of time that the medication is effective. One could not cure a broken arm with aspirin, and with any serious problem there is always the possibility that by masking the pain, one is not helping the problem.

There is now a climate of opinion in medical circles that tranquillizers are generally only beneficial on a very short-term basis, and only in cases where people are so incapacitated that they cannot carry on with their lives. They are, in any case, unlikely to derive further benefit from staying on tranquillizers longer than two or three weeks. It has been found that some people suffer a feeling of anxiety when taken off such medication, which in itself may be a withdrawal symptom, but which causes them to request a repeat prescription. Longer use of this medication can cause other withdrawal symptoms, for example 'pins and needles' and muscular stiffness. It does seem best therefore to face up to one's feelings as soon as possible and avoid reliance on medication, which may simply cause additional problems. At the moment there are few organizations dealing specifically with the problem of addiction to tranquillizers. If you do have a problem, your doctor may be able to refer you to a support group in your area, or you can write to the addresses on pages 150–1 for information.

Breast-feeding mothers

Another problem to be dealt with at the earliest opportunity is the discomfort experienced by the nursing mother, and this may be underestimated by the Casualty staff and others. When I asked Nurse J. if the hospital would be able to help the mother with problems caused by breast feeding, she replied that she could not guarantee that they would think of it. She was under the impression that the shock of the bereavement would cause the milk to dry up fairly quickly, and she felt that probably the Casualty doctor would find it inappropriate to enquire whether or not the mother was breast feeding, when she had just been told that her baby was dead. Nurse J. felt this was the sort of problem that should be dealt with by the GP, who would know the family, and that, therefore, he should be contacted by the hospital as soon as possible.

In Jane's case, the doctor who saw her after the bereavement was not able to help, only advising her to take proprietary pain-killers. After three days, she was helped by the local midwife who showed her how to bind her breasts which made it a little easier. However, she remembers those first few days as a time when both mental and physical pain were very bad.

Opinions amongst medical advisers vary and it will depend very much on your own doctor's feelings, whether or not you are prescribed medication. Even when referring specifically to a particular medication (Parladel) the doctors I spoke to disagreed as to the length of time it should be prescribed and to the necessity of prescribing it, and in fact, one pharmacist recommended a completely different medication (Estrovis) that required only two tablets to be taken.

Dr G. stressed the importance of mentioning the problem in the first place, or as soon as it becomes a problem, for it may not be at the forefront of the doctor's mind.

One has to remember to think of this – the mother may well forget. Also, to some extent, the doctor may not always think of these small problems in the rush of the larger problems. The shock of an unexpected death is experienced by the doctor as well. He doesn't expect to have babies die. It's a blow, and sometimes you forget the smaller problem in the larger problem of 'What caused the death, and was I responsible as a doctor?' So these things get forgotten.

Lynne, whose baby died aged three weeks, confirmed that she had to seek this help for herself. She rang her Health Visitor the morning after the baby's death, having experienced a night without feeding the baby. The Health Visitor called on the doctor herself, and he then prescribed some tablets. She was glad to have been given them so that the lactation period was not prolonged.

Only the GP can prescribe medication, but advice can be obtained from the Health Visitor, or even the District Midwife, if you are still in contact with her. Mrs E., a midwife attached to a hospital, confirmed that if the cessation of breast feeding (in other circumstances) was causing quite a severe problem in any of her patients, she would normally refer them to the GP and ask if he could prescribe medication. In general, however, there is a tendency to advise that the milk is not stopped in that way. Sometimes after the milk is stopped, it comes back and this can be very distressing. This can happen even at a later stage, because the milk supply is so well established. Mrs E. felt that it was better to let one's own body do the 'shutting down', in a more natural way, although it might prolong the period of lactation, so that there was no likelihood of it returning.

Health Visitor, Miss S., also felt that the natural way of stopping breast milk was best in view of the possible side-effects of many kinds of medication (which are all hormone based.) She felt that given the right advice and support, it should not present too many problems.

General advice can be summed up as follows:

1 Wear a tight, well supporting bra;
2 Reduce fluid intake;
3 Take paracetamol/aspirin every four to six hours (if necessary);
4 Do not handle the breasts (or express the milk).

I was more fortunate than Jane, for although I was also not given any form of medication, I experienced moderate discomfort rather than extreme pain. I was advised to cut down on fluid, which I did, and to express a little milk, if it helped. I did this initially, but found it an uncomfortable and demoralizing task, and after a day or so stopped doing it, preferring the discomfort to the action of pouring away the milk that had been meant for my baby. I continued to wear a National Childbirth Trust nursing bra (the tightness of which can be adjusted) which was probably helpful, and I did not feel the need to take pain-killers. But in a way, I felt that the nagging, physical difficulties were an irrelevance to the real mental torture, whereas to some mothers they served to accentuate it. In my case, it took a full week for the milk to disappear completely, thus belying any assumption that the milk supply would dry up in a couple of days because of the effect of the shock upon the bereaved mother. Other mothers mentioned in Sylvia Limerick's survey experienced problems for up to two weeks.

In this survey, Lady Limerick mentions that some women were helped psychologically by donating breast milk to the neonatal baby unit of the local hospital, although this obviously conflicts with advice not to handle the breasts or to express milk. Some mothers may feel that it is essential to them that the milk dries up as soon as possible, and that acceptance of their baby's death is incomplete until this residue from the baby's life is ended. However, the Foundation leaflet giving advice to GPs suggests that milk can be expressed once a day if an easy method is available. If the mother finds it comforting to know that her milk is being used, and a relief to do this, it should not greatly extend the time before the milk dries up.

Midwife, Mrs E., felt that in the normal circumstances of a mother ceasing to breast feed, it was always preferable to do so gradually. In these special circumstances, she felt it might be helpful to mothers to donate their milk to neonatal baby units, if it was suitable, and if the mothers were able to continue for a week to ten days, their discomfort might be considerably reduced. It would not be necessary for the mother to empty the breasts totally, but to give enough to make her comfortable. This way she would not be over-stimulating the supply and thus prolonging it.

However, this suggestion is one that should come from the mother and no one else. Perhaps the GP can assist the mother in this endeavour, if she believes it will be therapeutic, for she may not feel strong enough to instigate it herself. However, it is certainly not an idea that should be thrust upon her. At this stage of the tragedy, she may not feel able to give anything of herself to anyone else. I am not at all convinced that I would have been capable of doing it myself, had anyone suggested it to me. Similarly, Lynne felt that she could not have done it.

In her survey, Lady Limerick mentions that over 8 per cent of mothers had complained strongly of inadequate help with the problems of engorgement of the breasts. Apart from not prescribing tablets, one doctor mentioned had not even given the most basic advice, i.e. to cut down on fluids.

One can see that there are circumstances in which it may not occur to the doctor that the mother is in great discomfort unless she tells him. One can also see that the mother may not, in the shock of the moment, think to mention the problem to the doctor initially. But once she has made it clear to the doctor that she is in pain, there is absolutely no excuse for him to regard it as a triviality, even though he knows it will disappear on its own during the next week to fortnight. It is, as Dr G. said, 'a very painful reminder, both physically and emotionally'.

The death of one twin

If the baby that dies is one of twins, the parents may be very concerned for their surviving baby. In view of the increased risk of cot death in twins, it is sometimes helpful if the surviving twin can be taken into hospital for observation for a few days.

Transplant surgery

Some parents may wish to donate their baby's organs, eyes or body, so that others might benefit.

Maureen A. remembered that a couple of weeks after her son's death, she had remarked to the Health Visitor that no one had even suggested that his eyes might have been used so that a baby born blind might have benefited. Maureen B. would have approved of transplant surgery, and Sue and Neville were very much in favour of it, emphasizing that they and their daughter all carry donor cards now.

Parents may wonder, therefore, why no such request is made to them, or why their offer, if they should think of making that offer, is refused.

It is always difficult for doctors to put this sort of request to anyone suddenly bereaved. However, when someone dies at home, the delay before they reach the hospital is probably too long for transplant surgery to be carried out. Dr G. explained to me that organ donation is most often appropriate in the case of injury deaths, under hospital conditions where there is a very little time-gap between the death of the patient and the beginning of the operation.

In the helpful leaflet, 'What to do after a death', issued by the Department of Social Security, it states that heart, liver or kidneys must be removed within half an hour of death, and the corneas from the eyes within twelve hours. In the case of an unexpected undiagnosed death, the law must take precedence, a post-mortem examination must be carried out, and this further delay means that donation of the baby's organs is not a practical proposition. Furthermore, a body will not be accepted for medical teaching purposes if a post-mortem has taken place.

Photographs

At this stage, or some time before the funeral is held, it may come into the parents' minds that they have no photographs of their baby. All the parents I spoke to had, at the time of their baby's death, already had photographs taken, or taken them themselves. Nevertheless, not everyone thinks about photographs during the first month of a baby's life, and it may be that some parents are left without this reminder of their baby. Some parents I spoke to felt it would be macabre to suggest that photographs be taken of the dead baby. Yet, those parents left without other photographs might find them a comfort to have and perhaps this could be organized at the Chapel of Rest.

There has been discussion in recent years of the benefits to parents of having photographs taken of their still-born babies, so that they have something positive they can retain. As I pointed out earlier, there are differences in reactions to a still birth and to a cot death but, nevertheless, I believe that parents without photographs of their baby of a few weeks or months old might feel an added deprivation at not having these personal reminders.

However, as with much of the advice in this chapter, there is no right or wrong way of doing things. Parents need to be shown the choices open to them and then to be allowed to make their own decision. Without previous experience of such traumatic events, parents need to be given permission to follow their own instincts.

2 The first week

Official procedures

Some time during the first or second day, certain official procedures must be carried out and actions taken. Some of the procedures set out here apply only to England and Wales.* There is a logical sequence of events, which very often will be explained by those people involved, i.e. the doctor/hospital, the police, the Coroner's officer, the Registrar and/or the funeral directors, so do ask for their help and advice. One or more of these officials may know of or have literature from the main support group for the parents of cot death victims, the Foundation for the Study of Infant Deaths. In addition, the leaflet, 'What to do after a death' can be obtained from the Department of Social Security and copies may be available from some of the official sources mentioned above.

Visit by the police or Coroner's officer

Parents are often willing to go back over the previous hours before their baby's death and answer detailed questions, in the hope that their answers may reveal some clue as to the reason for the mysterious death. Nevertheless, it comes as a shock to many parents to find that the police will have to be involved, and either they, or the Coroner's officer, who is usually a civilian, are likely to call at the house and may wish to see the baby's room and bedding. Their very presence makes the parents feel that there is something to feel guilty about.

Neville remembers being slightly irritated by the police

* In Scotland, sudden deaths are investigated by the Procurator Fiscal.

questions, though he recognized that they had a job to do. With hindsight, he felt that they had carried out the questioning to the best of their ability.

Maureen and Rod were prepared in advance by the police, who arrived at the hospital while they were there, and told them that they would be calling to interview them at home later in the same day. When the police arrived, they examined the bedding and asked what had happened. When they left, the GP who was waiting in the car outside came in. Maureen felt that was a considerate action.

Lynne, too, was prepared by a policewoman for their susequent call, and was also told by her that there would be a post-mortem and an inquest.

In my case, I did not see the police when they called to see the bedding, since I was still at the hospital. When I heard of their visit, I immediately feared the worst: that there would be an inquest and that I would be accused of negligence of some sort.

In fact, a police officer or the Coroner's officer attends at all cases of sudden death in the community, for it has to be established that the sudden death is a natural death, and that there are no signs of a deliberate act by any persons. This procedure is carried out in order to reveal the very occasional cases of infanticide or baby battering that may initially appear to be cot deaths, and therefore to protect the innocent parents by exonerating them. Where there is doubt, there may be an inquest, but in the majority of cases of cot death, there is no doubt, and the post-mortem examination verifies the hospital or doctor's initial reaction that a natural death has occurred.

Although under such circumstances no inquest need take place, according to Sylvia Limerick's survey, in 10 to 12 per cent of cot deaths during the preceding few years, inquests did take place, though some of these were carried out by certain Coroners, simply as a matter of routine, and did not imply suspicion of the parents. In some areas, this practice has now ceased.

The Coroner

Whether or not it is the local GP or a hospital doctor who has proclaimed the baby dead, he is almost certain to report the death to the Coroner (who is a doctor or lawyer responsible for investigating certain types of death), for the following reason or reasons:

1 The death was sudden and unexpected;
2 The baby may not have been seen by a doctor during the previous fourteen days; and/or
3 The cause of the death was uncertain.

The Coroner will probably arrange for a post-mortem examination and this should, from the point of view of accuracy of diagnosis, be carried out as soon as possible. The parents too, of course, will want to know the verdict as soon as they can. The Coroner will in most cases issue a Pink Form B for the Registrar of Births and Deaths, when the examination has shown that death was due to natural causes, and he has exercised his discretion not to hold an inquest. If he does decide to hold an inquest, there may be some delay. However, in this event, authorization can be given for the funeral to take place in advance of the inquest. If no inquest is to take place, the Coroner or his officer will usually inform the parents or their doctor of the cause of death and they can then go to register the death of the baby. The Coroner will either send Pink Form B direct to the Registrar or give it to the parents to take with them. The parents will have been asked early on, by the Coroner's officer, if they wish to have their dead baby cremated, since the Coroner issues the certificate for cremation. The Registrar will register the death and he is then able to let the parents have a copy of the Death Certificate at a cost of £2 (1989) and a Disposal certificate for burial if needed, enabling the parents to arrange for the baby's burial or cremation. He will also supply a Certificate of Registration of Death (form BD8), which will be required by the Department of Social Security, if financial help is needed to pay for the funeral. This help is available if you are already receiving certain benefits.

The cause of death

Many of the parents I spoke to were told verbally that their baby's death was a cot death, or Sudden Infant Death Syndrome. However, very often, it was nevertheless shown on the death certificate as a more complicated name or as a virus.

Death certificate

The parents can obtain additional copies of the Death Certificate at £2 each. It might be useful to take at least one extra copy (or obtain a photocopy). If the certificate is passed on, the parents have no further record, and in subsequent weeks, they may wish to refer to it, particularly if the wording of the cause of death is something other than just 'cot death' or SIDS. They may also need to show evidence of the death, if, for example, a bank account or similar has been opened in the baby's name. (In these circumstances the Death Certificate would subsequently be returned to the parents.) Therefore parents may feel that it is worth having an extra copy that they can refer to. Copies of the Death Certificate obtained at a later date will cost £5.

Post-mortem report

Parents may also wish to see a copy of the post-mortem report, and at the present time, parents in England and Wales are entitled to this under the 1984 Coroners' Rules, though there may be a small fee, currently 55p per page. I regretted not having an extra copy of the Death Certificate, nor a copy of the post-mortem report to which I could refer, not immediately, but when I was recovered sufficiently to want to know more about the factors that had added up to my daughter's death.

If, even at a later stage, you wish to have a copy of the post-mortem report, you can ask your doctor, who will be able to contact the Coroner on your behalf. The Coroner will send the report direct to the doctor, who will then explain it to you. Alternatively, you could also contact the Coroner's office direct. Records are kept for quite a long time, certainly at least six years, and parents wishing to have this report many years afterwards have still been able to obtain it. Parents at a Study Day held by the Foundation for the Study of Infant Deaths quoted instances of obtaining post-mortem reports as long as thirteen years after their baby's death.

If the records are still in existence, but parents nevertheless meet with difficulties, they may wish to contact The Coroner's Society for assistance. Their address is shown at the end of the book.

Informing others

As I have already said, if the baby was discovered late at night, it may not be until the following morning that some of the procedures, and other actions concerning the family, get under way. This was the case with my husband Michael and myself, and in fact we shared the agony of the first night with no one else and awoke after our fitful and disturbed sleep to the grim task of informing relatives and friends.

Those people who found their babies in the early part of the day obviously wished to contact those close to them on the same day, and many of those parents I spoke to did indeed get immediate support from close friends or neighbours.

It was Michael who telephoned the majority of our relatives and friends. It is a task that I would have found very difficult and I could not have avoided breaking down. In the small village in which I live, where the local shopkeepers tend to know their customers, I also found it helpful to ask the Health Visitor, when she came for the first time on the day after Amanda's death, to call in at these shops and tell them what had happened. This way, I could at least avoid the painful situation of being asked when I went in there, 'How's the baby?' Similarly, the policeman who interviewed Maureen and Rod told their neighbours on their behalf.

Where possible, of course, friends can contact others on your behalf and close relatives can inform more distant ones. This is always a help to the parents and most people are happy to help in this small way.

Announcement in the press

Those parents who announced the birth of their child in the local or daily press would be sensible to put an announcement of the death in the same paper, knowing that the information would at least be likely to reach the same people as the previous notification. My sister- and brother-in-law offered to do this for us and this was very helpful, since it was certainly not the sort of thing we would have thought of in the initial few days. It meant that a wider circle of people were notifed and cut down some of the potentially hurtful and embarrassing moments that might have occurred later on.

The Identification

It is possible that one parent or other will be required to attend an identification, though why this seemingly unnecessary formality had to be carried out I certainly could not understand at the time of my daugher's death. It is still a requirement in the event of an inquest being held, which can only be decided later by the Coroner. However, in some areas, the fact that one or both of the parents has accompanied the baby to hospital is considered sufficient to obviate the need for any formal identification.

Michael and I went together to the identification and we were shown Amanda behind a glass screen. I remember that the Coroner's officer introduced us to the mortician and implied that he had done well in improving her appearance. As I did not know how she would otherwise have looked, I thanked him, as appeared to be expected, but in fact it had been an ordeal to see her, certainly not a comfort. She had a strange grimace on her face, and though the sight of her when we first discovered her was bad enough, this second vision was worse.

When Michael was asked to attend at the mortuary, I chose to go with him, since I was very reluctant to be left in the house on my own. I was not afraid; I just found it unbearable to be left with my own thoughts at that stage. It happened that the Coroner's officer chose this occasion to ask us the details of Amanda's death, which he incorporated into a statement. In this respect, it was helpful that I was there, although in some of the families that I spoke to, the husband went alone to carry out the identification.

It does seem that there is a great deal of running around and organizing to do in the first two or three days. It sounds belittling of death itself to say that if you have already experienced the death of someone close, the knowledge of the procedures to be carried out is helpful. However, for some parents it is their first encounter with death, and for them, the complications of organizing and co-ordinating the visits to the Coroner and Registrar and arrangements with the Funeral Directors are an added burden. Whatever pressure can be lifted by these officials must be helpful.

Once Jane and David were in touch with the hospital, they were given the telephone number of the Compassionate Friends (an organization that counsels the bereaved parents of children of all ages); they were told that a post-mortem would be necessary, but that it would not take place until after the weekend. The hospital made arrangements for Jane and David to see the consultant paediatrician the next morning, which was Sunday. The paediatrician then explained the procedures to them; that there would be a post-mortem the next day, and that once the result was known, they would have to get the Death Certificate and they could arrange for a funeral. Their local vicar was extremely helpful; he came to see them later on Sunday and offered to contact an undertaker for them. He explained the situation to the undertaker, who then contacted them direct. This made things easier than if they had had to do that themselves, since the undertaker only needed to verify small details with them.

Maureen and Rod were told by their doctor that there would be a post-mortem. Then the police, who had to report back to the Coroner's office whether a burial or cremation would be taking place, gave them the names of some undertakers, since they had no idea who to contact. Lynne and Paul chose the funeral directors who had carried out the arrangements for the funeral of Lynne's mother, who had died some years before. The funeral directors were extremely kind, and, as was their policy when dealing with the death of a baby, they made only the statutory crematorium charge, adding only an amount to cover the cost of the coffin and flowers, but nothing for their own services.

Sue and Neville were also impressed that because of the nature of the community in which they lived, the bill for their funeral was not presented to them until a year after the death.

Funeral directors

How does one go about choosing a firm of funeral directors? Parents might rely upon their own past experience, like Lynne and Paul, or alternatively, someone else's recommendation. If the baby was declared dead at home, the Coroner will have decided (sometimes on a rota basis) which funeral director should be called to the house to remove the baby to hospital for the post-mortem (unless the family have requested the use of a particular funeral director). Parents might decide to use this same person to arrange the funeral. There is a National Association of Funeral Directors and parents may wish to seek a company from amongst their members. 'Not every company is obliged to be a member of this organization, but many who wish to keep standards up and to have a professional approach do join it and are bound by a very strict code of conduct,' I was told by Mr S., a funeral director.

A good funeral director will be a great asset. If necessary, mourners could pass the whole responsibility on to him. He might be called upon to contact the minister of religion on behalf of the parents, for not everyone knows the name of the parish minister. He could, if required, deal with all the arrangements, the church, cemetery, crematorium, organist or choir. He might in addition be able to advise the couple who they can turn to for counselling, or put them in touch with other bereaved parents.

Sometimes people have wishes that they feel might be regarded as silly. Mr S. said that parents should not be shy about making such wishes clear to the funeral director. Some small, niggling worry, for example about the clothes they wish the baby to wear, may be easily sorted out, or the parents may be reassured that a particular arrangement is able to be carried out.

Possibly, close friends or relations – perhaps one or other set of grandparents – want to take the pressure off the young couple, by taking over the organization of the funeral, but this is not necessarily a good thing. The process of coming to terms with the death begins with both parents working through the various aspects of the baby's death. I believe that this 'journey of acceptance' must be travelled, without taking short cuts. The couple need to travel it together, as a team, and attempts by outsiders (and I include grandparents, in this particular context) to remove all the painful tasks are likely to be damaging.

Initially, after a particularly harrowing bereavement, the mourners go through a stage of passivity, where they allow (and are grateful for) things to be done for them or to them, but gradually they wish to be more active themselves. In the case of the death of a young baby, it is quite possible that the husband may arrive at this 'active' stage somewhat earlier than his wife. In this case, the organizing of the funeral is a practical way for him to express his grief, whilst relieving his wife of the burden. Later, there will be jobs that are bound to fall to his wife to do, and which it is unlikely to be practical for the husband to carry out.

I was very glad that Michael took on the entire burden of organizing the funeral, for I remember that during the first two or three days after Amanda's death, even the smallest task like making a bed or cooking a meal seemed to need an enormous physical effort from me.

Neville took on all the responsibility of the funeral and other arrangements after baby Anthony's death. It was he who was told of the necessary formalities and he did not involve Sue, who was heavily drugged, in the details of the arrangements. Neville was, in any case, aware of the procedures, since his father had died only three years earlier. During the weeks that followed their baby's death, and before the cremation, there were a number of things to be done. He had to keep in touch with the office, though he did not go in; there were people to talk to, appointments to change, as well as dealing with the funeral arrangements. In addition, their daughter of two-and-a-half had to be occupied.

The children

If there are any children in the house, they need to be told of the death of their brother or sister without delay in a way that is appropriate to their age and to any previous discussions of death that may have taken place in the home.

Some parents want to pass on a religious idea to their children. Lynne felt that she needed guidance from someone other than her family, who were all too closely involved, so she went to her Rector and talked to him about it. Lynne was worried because the baby had not been christened and the Rector told her that he did not think that God would turn him away for that reason; he drew her attention to the picture, 'Suffer little children to come unto Me,' and she found this a comforting idea to pass on to her son. Later she bought the picture.

Sue and Neville explained to their daughter Tracey that the baby had been very ill, and she *was* able to comprehend illness, since both her grandmothers had been ill recently. Her parents explained that though doctors could normally make people better, there were some occasions when they could not cure people, and this was one of those occasions. They told her that the doctors had tried very hard, they had not succeeded and had taken the baby away, and the baby was not coming back.

Maureen and Rod's two-year-old son Nicholas had gone with his parents to the hospital when the baby was found dead, and he had been left with a nurse when they were taken to see the baby in the chapel. He was aware that something was wrong, and when they returned, he was crying, though this was unusual for him. However, he was confused because his brother Timothy had been in hospital before and he did not understand that the situation was not the same as previously, when Timothy had come home after his stay in hospital, and thought that his baby brother would come out some other day. 'We don't have any religious faith and so we had simply to explain it to him as best we could, and to say that no, he wasn't coming back.'

However, Mrs S., a Child Guidance Social Worker, expressed to me reservations about telling a child that the baby had gone away and was not coming back and felt that in a young child, this might make them fearful of any sort of journey and afraid that people were going to go away and not come back.

Maureen felt uneasy about telling Nicholas that the baby had gone to live with Jesus. Even apart from her lack of religious feelings, she felt that Nicholas might misinterpret the explanation and feel that his parents had not treated the baby well and so he had chosen to go and live somewhere else.

I have subsequently heard somebody say they thought it was a very bad idea to say that dying was like going to sleep. We did actually say that to Nicholas and he just once said 'But I *will* wake up, won't I?' so we said, 'Yes, you will!'

But it was a very long process of explanation.

We found it very difficult to explain something for which we had no satisfactory explanation ourselves. I had actually thought beforehand how I could explain, for example, the death of a grandparent and how I would explain that all things went through a natural cycle, like the flowers in the garden and the leaves on the trees, and at the end of the life, that was the end of it. We thought this was quite a nice satisfactory explanation. Of course, it doesn't work for a baby.

Mrs S. said that you have to explain things very simply to a young child. She herself had been able to reassure a child who had experienced a still birth in the family, by saying that it was not quite the right time for the baby to come; it had decided that it was too soon, and had come a bit later after all (when, in fact, another baby had been born). Mrs S. said that this explanation had seemed appropriate in that particular case, although not necessarily in other cases. Since it is important for mothers themselves to differentiate between the dead baby and any future child, I was not totally happy with the implication that the same child had been reborn at a later date.

Nevertheless, in the same way as one might say that people eventually became too old to function properly in the world, as parents may have already explained to their children, or as Maureen A. had envisaged, so one could pass on the idea that at the beginning of life, sometimes the baby was not quite strong enough or big enough to face the world.

Mrs S. also suggested that in an effort to remove from the remaining child the fear of being struck down in some way by some external force, it would be quite sensible to put more responsibility on the baby itself – that is, to suggest that the baby *decided* it was not ready to live here.

Between the ages of three and five, many children are extremely fearful of real and imaginary terrors. Perhaps, if they have in the past expressed a fear of death, you may have already told them that only old people die, so they may be very disturbed at the death of a young baby. I think that, even if the children do not express their fears, almost as soon as you are able to discuss the death with them, you must act to relieve their worry that they too may suddenly die, or that they will lose either of their parents.

It may be that in the emotion of the moment, an unconsidered statement is blurted out. Initially, all I said to my son was, 'Our baby died in the night' – and then burst into tears. Subsequently, however, I told him that only old people and very ill people die, and that the baby was very ill with a disease that only babies have, although we had not realized it at the time.

Marian and John's children, whose ages ranged from seven to ten years, were concerned in a practical way. John told them that baby Victoria had gone to heaven and this prompted them to ask if Jesus would feed the baby, and if she would grow in heaven. They were also particularly concerned that she might have suffered, and he assured them that she did not suffer in any way, but that she went to sleep and did not wake up. Aware that this might make them afraid of going to sleep, he, like me, assured them that it only happened to little babies.

In spite of my efforts to reassure my son, I was myself quite irrationally concerned about him, though I did not allow him to be aware of that. I reinforced my statement more than once over the next few months, but it is important to remember that children's worries start as soon as they are aware of the death of their brother or sister.

Since the majority of parents are young, and since, in most cases, there will have been no previous need for such explanations to the children, there is no reason for parents to be skilled at such a job, or to blame themselves for doing it badly. According to Mrs S., even in cases where parents fail to tell the children the truth, the likelihood is that the children will sum up the situation and realize what has happened. Because they are often more astute than we realize, they are probably aware of their parents' difficulties in telling them of the tragedy; and because of their protective feelings towards their parents, they may keep up the pretence of not knowing. However, it is kinder not to place that burden upon the child, and best if parents tell the children as near as they can get to the truth as they see it, without worrying the children with their own irrational fears. Parents will then be able to repeat that explanation in the coming months, for they will almost certainly be called upon for reassurance over and over again.

Children may also worry because they imagine that their bad feelings towards the baby, who usurped their position in the family, have contributed to, or caused the baby's death. If the parents are preoccupied, or the children are sent away, they may consider they are being punished for this supposed wickedness. Two-year-olds in particular are at a very vulnerable age and are likely to be hurt if apparently abandoned into the care of someone else, so it is perhaps important to keep them within the family, as far as possible. As far as older children are concerned, some parents feel it is best to keep to the normal routine as far as possible. Our instincts, on the morning after Amanda's death, were to arrange for our son of nearly four years old to go to play-school as usual. Friends took him there and offered to look after him for the rest of the day, and I believe they may even have taken him for outings with their own children on a few other occasions during that week.

Of course, it is not right to exclude children from an important event in the family, whether happy or sad, and it was not our intention to do this. Our son did not stay away overnight and I made no attempt to hide my grief from him, when he was at home. In addition, later I talked to him about the tragedy, in a simple way. The problem during the first week is that the mother, who is usually the person involved in the care of the child or other children of the family, may be so shocked that she is almost incapable of doing anything for anyone, irrespective of whether or not she has been sedated.

In addition, one is likely to take the least line of resistance. If someone offers to take the children to the circus, for example, it is difficult to summon up the will-power to refuse such an offer, even though in the long run it might be better for all the family to share in the tragedy from the very beginning. There is also the possibility that the mother may feel that she should not allow herself to be too possessive of the surviving child.

However, it is important to make the situation quite clear to the child, by saying something like: 'As you know, we are very sad, because our baby has died. We don't want you to be sad all the time, so we thought you might like to go with Uncle and Auntie, for an afternoon out.' I have always tried to tell my children the truth, even if it was in a simplistic way, and this would have been a fairly accurate statement of my feelings at that time.

Mrs S. suggested to me that if the mother simply could not cope at that early stage, it would be helpful to arrange for a 'substitute mother' to give a little extra attention to the child or children. If that person, perhaps an aunt or grandmother, could come into the home, the child would not feel it was being sent away and could still participate in the life of the family, such as it was.

We ought to try to imagine what children are actually thinking and that may guide us as to the things we should be saying to them. The understanding of the situation will broaden and change, of course, according to the age of the child. I remember as a ten-year-old being left with friends on the day when my aunt died of cancer. I remember their attempts to cheer me up, which were transparently obvious to a child of that age. Possibly the other children of the family will be somewhat younger than I was then, and they will not yet have achieved that degree of sophistication. However, even when they are six or seven, it is important not to underestimate their ability to comprehend the situation and their desire to share in it.

Post-mortem examination and after

Once the post-mortem verdict has been given and the arrangements are under way, parents may once again be in a dilemma as to whether or not to see the dead baby again. On the night of her death, I had held Amanda for the entire period from our discovery of her, until the arrival of the ambulance men. When they took her from my arms, I felt that I had held her for the last time. I said my goodbye to her then.

However, in some circumstances, parents, particularly those who had no opportunity earlier to say goodbye, may want to see the baby before the funeral takes place, and it is their right to do so. The funeral director may, in fact, ask if they wish to see the baby again before the funeral, and if the answer is yes, may also ask for clothes and a bonnet in which to dress the baby. It may be helpful if parents are warned of what they should expect to see, so that they are not too shaken by their experience. In addition, most parents do not know in what condition their baby will be after the post-mortem examination.

Maureen A. had assumed that she would not have been able to see the baby after the post-mortem.

I had terrible visions of him being cut up in such an awful way that it would not be possible. I'm a bit sorry in a way that I didn't see him again at the undertakers, but talking to other people who have seen older people and also babies again, they seem to have changed so much that it wasn't a comfort.

Her husband Rod had found that changes had already taken place in the baby's colouring when he went to identify him.

I asked Dr G. to explain to me what happened at the post-mortem examination, and whether the baby was operated on, and then returned to its 'normal' state. I was told that it is a major operation and that the organs are kept for microscopic examination, but the rest are re-inserted in the body which is sewn up again, and then the child is usually dressed. I asked if the child would be in an acceptable state to be seen again by the parents before the funeral.

Yes, the face is not affected; the limbs are not affected; there would be an operational scar in the centre of the tummy; and the brain, of course, may well be examined, so there would be an operational scar on the head. So it would be customary, when preparing the baby for the funeral, to put on some kind of bonnet. It sounds gruesome, but when it's finished, in fact, it's often difficult to tell, unless you were to undress the baby.

However, Dr C. pointed out that the body is quite frequently discoloured, bluish, almost as if it is bruised, so it could be distressing to a parent.

Maureen B., who did not feel she had said goodbye to her baby Michelle, visited the Chapel of Rest with her husband Tony, who had been away at the time of Michelle's death, but she did not feel she had benefited from the visit. The baby looked like a doll with white face and purple lips. It no longer seemed to be her baby, and even when the funeral took place, and for some time afterwards, this distorted memory remained with her.

Jane and David were given the opportunity of seeing baby Naomi in the Chapel of Rest, but they declined the offer. Although in retrospect, Jane felt that she would have liked to have had a chance to see Naomi again before the funeral, she did not think she would have wanted to have seen her daughter in the coffin. So she did not regret that decision.

To a certain extent, the baby's appearance may be determined by the expertise of the funeral director. Mr S. told me that in his company, a temporary preservation treatment is carried out in all cases, by qualified staff. Sometimes this is in the form of an arterial injection (though this is particularly difficult in the case of babies). This has the effect of delaying any deterioration in the dead person's appearance and giving it a more natural look.

Mr S. felt that many parents could get a great deal of comfort out of coming to see the dead baby at the chapel, and he thought that the comfort might well outweigh the apprehension felt by the parents. He also quoted instances where parents had come to the chapel to sit there for a while with the closed coffin, without seeing the baby, and they too had seemed to derive benefit from that.

The funeral

Costs

For a young couple who are unprepared for a sudden large expenditure, the funeral is a financial blow, and many families are rather shocked to find that the funeral costs for a baby are not much less than for an adult.

Mr S. pointed out that his company would provide a hearse, a limousine for the family if required, and the use of the chapel for them to visit the baby if they wanted. It was likely that just as much time was spent by the funeral director preparing for a baby's funeral as for an adult's.

In some cases, there is a grave fee, as well as the grave-digging fee and the minister's fee. The latter is actually part of the minister's salary, so for him to waive his fee is a personal sacrifice, though some ministers do so nevertheless.

A good funeral director would also be sympathetic to the problems of young parents with limited financial resources. However, if either partner is already in receipt of certain Social Security benefits, they may be entitled to receive help from the Social Fund towards the cost of a simple funeral. In this case, application should be made to a Social Security office, but general advice can also be obtained from Freeline Social Security, 0800 666555. If the parents do not come into this category, but still cannot afford the cost of the funeral, then the local authority will bury the child in a common grave. Sadly, in such cases, the grave cannot be marked, and no memorial stone or plaque can be erected. However, Mr S. recommended that parents ask the funeral director for assistance before using this last resort. Sometimes, funeral directors know of a charity or trust which will be able to help in such a case.

In Mr S.'s own company, as in the case of the funeral directors who carried out Lynne's baby's funeral, there was a policy to cut costs to the minimum in the case of a child, sometimes even sustaining a financial loss. Mr S. said he would be very reluctant to send parents away because of financial difficulties; if they told him what they could afford he would do his best to help them. Members of the National Association are obliged to offer a basic funeral, but parents sometimes ask for a grand funeral, thinking it is expected of them, when they cannot actually afford it.

A cremation is cheaper than a burial, but parents tend to choose what feels right for them.

The Foundation for the Study of Infant Deaths has submitted full details of the costs of infants' funerals to the Department of Social Security and copies of their analysis can be obtained from the Foundation.

A comfort to the family

How much parents benefit from the funeral service seems to me to depend to a certain extent on the religious feelings that they already have.

Jane felt that the funeral was very helpful to both her and her husband David. In some ways, however, she said that it was the worst part of the next few days. It took place six days after Naomi's death and after four days she was aware of it 'looming up' over her.

Maureen A. too spoke of the burden of the waiting period. 'It was like waiting for an exam, and wishing it was all over with. I think that it was such an ordeal that I was really quite grateful for the oblivion [of sedatives].'

Maureen and Rod, who have no religious beliefs, did not find the funeral helpful at all, and they were glad when it was over. In retrospect, Maureen was sad too that the crematorium service was conducted by someone entirely unknown to her.

I remember being apprehensive about Amanda's funeral, yet when it took place, I found it an extremely comforting experience. The ritual, which is a part of my religion, the Jewish religion, was welcomingly familiar, at a time when everything else was alien and unfamiliar.

Mandy, whose baby Sophie had died tragically on Christmas Eve, wrote movingly of the week leading up to her baby's funeral.

The first week after Sophie's death was simply horrific; a feeling of sheer desolation and of being in a long black tunnel, not wanting to eat or even live. I remember not caring if it was day or night and simply just drifting until the funeral. Another black day, and my worst memory was that of a small man carrying Sophie's miniscule coffin, all by himself. I think the whole family found that a dreadfully pathetic sight.

Unexpectedly, when the service started, I found things easier to bear, almost as if I was given an inner strength in order to cope with this tragic situation, and I walked out of church feeling a lot easier than when I had gone in.

One thing that was comforting to me was to have my family around at the funeral. Perhaps this was partly because I had moved away from them since my marriage, and to be surrounded by them once again was in some way a return to the comfort of childhood. In addition, however, I was perhaps unduly concerned that my family should pay their respects to Amanda (many of them without knowing her), and not behave as if her death was less important than that of an older person.

My feelings on this matter were not shared by Maureen and Rod, who felt that they could not stop people coming to their baby's funeral, but would have preferred no one to come, so that they could have escaped the burden of organizing other people. Their parents had only seen Timothy as a very tiny baby and he had changed somewhat, during the nine weeks of his life. Maureen and Rod really felt they were the only people who knew what he was like when he died and that therefore they were the only ones who had any purpose to be at the funeral.

Jane, too, said that it was of no consequence to her whether relations attended or whether she and David were there on their own. She was not interested in the details of the funeral; she felt it would be of emotional benefit to her, and the details of arrangements were unimportant to her.

In view of the diverse feelings of parents, it might be helpful if the family could tactfully enquire what the parents would prefer.

For me, the familiarity of the service and its unchanging nature was helpful. However, in her Management Survey, Sylvia Limerick mentions that a small percentage of parents had a special service, or a non-religious service.

Sue and Neville, who are of different faiths, said that their local vicar had carried out an 'ecumenical service'. He had been particularly sensitive to their needs, since his own grandchild had died the previous year. His service was moving and appropriate and they had all cried. However, Neville said the funeral had no significant bearing on the death as far as he was concerned; it had to be done, and the sooner it was done the better. The point of significance for him was the discovery of the baby.

Nevertheless, the ability to express one's grief can be more helpful than one realizes. In the first few days, parents are numbed and shocked. Sometimes, in this first shock, people carry on functioning mechanically, almost coldly, without giving expression to their grief. The funeral is, or should be, an opportunity to give vent to their feelings.

Jane (perhaps mindful of her father's funeral, which she had experienced six or seven years before), said that sometimes funerals could be very difficult, when there was an attitude of, 'We've got to get through the funeral; we mustn't break down; we must try and be strong.' However, Jane had no feeling that she had to keep a 'stiff upper lip', nor did she care what people thought. She felt the funeral had given her the chance to express her grief.

I think possibly in our society, that's what we've lost track of; because that's what they're for; if you watch other cultures having a funeral with all the wailing and gnashing of teeth, I can see the point of that; it cleans the spirit and helps.

In addition to this releasing of emotion, another function of the funeral is to demonstrate the finality of the death, although it may be that parents who see their babies after the death need no further statement of this fact. Yet instead of the baby's death being the end, there is a series of events that follow it, each one another ordeal in itself. The interviews with police and doctors, the identification, and the post-mortem are all added burdens during that miserable few days. With the exception of those unfortunate people who have to undergo an inquest, the funeral really does signal the end of these occurrences.

Sue commented:

I found it an end and a start. It was over. It put a full-stop on what had happened that previous week. It gave me a focal point of trying to start again. From that point of view, it was helpful. It wasn't spiritually helpful, because I don't know that I believe in God.

Jane reiterated those feelings:

It's like the psychological crossing. It is over, after the funeral. There's no more of it to come and you can start building upwards from rock bottom.

A memorial

For some people it is important that there is a permanent memorial that they can visit, and in the case of a burial, this need is satisfied by a marked grave. However, crematoria may vary in their attitude to the ashes of a baby; sometimes they are buried in a churchyard or sometimes in a Garden of Remembrance at the crematorium, in which case, the place will be known at the office of the crematorium. Under the Cremation Regulations parents must be informed in advance when it appears that no ashes will result from cremation. If they decide to go ahead with the cremation in spite of this, they may wish to record an entry in the Book of Remembrance, or have a bush planted as a memorial.

Taking children to the funeral

Most of the people I spoke to, whose children were under four or five years old, had refrained from taking them to the funeral, preferring to leave them with friends. It is very difficult to expose a young child to what one imagines will be a traumatic event. The idea of being buried in the ground, or burned, is frightening to a young imaginative child, and it might not be appropriate to take them to a funeral, until they are of an age to have knowledge through books or television of the events of a funeral. On the other hand, the Revd. Ron Robinson, who has spoken often at Foundation Study Days, has talked of his early years in the East End of London, when children were raised to be more 'comfortable' with death and, from about four years old, were automatically taken in to see dead relatives.

In Lady Limerick's Management Survey, she mentions that it may be beneficial for children from about the age of six to accompany the family to the funeral. Pam, herself the mother of older children, gave her children the choice. Her daughter, who was nearly eleven at the time of the death, decided to go to the funeral. However, it was not possible to tell whether it had helped, and she still reacted to the death without warning, about a month later, by dissolving into tears. Pam's son who was eight-and-a-half, did not want to go and went to school as usual.

Marian, at the time of her baby's death, had three children between seven and eleven. The funeral took the form of a service, followed by the burial in the local churchyard, which she felt would be too traumatic for the children. At Marian's church it was possible to have services taped, which was a comfort to Marian and her husband John. Some time after, they played the tape of the service to the children, when they felt they could 'handle' it. Chris, aged seven, who had shown his feelings most, at the time of the baby's death, was hardly affected by the funeral, but Timothy, ten, and Elizabeth, nearly nine, were very upset by it. Timothy, who had not shown outward signs of grief previously, and had obviously 'bottled it all up', was terribly upset, but was able to release his feelings for the first time. This gave Marian the opening to talk to him about the death.

It may be that once children are of an age to comprehend the family tragedy, they should be given an opportunity for an outward expression of grief. Pam, who is the organizer of a Foundation support group, has met with various views, including one mother whose two-year-old was taken, as a matter of course, to the baby's funeral, which was a cremation followed by the burial of ashes. It is possible that in keeping our children away from the funeral at a young age, we are assuming in them emotions that do not exist and imparting to them our own distaste and horror at the idea of death.

However, the benefits of including the child in the experience should be balanced against the child's possible fears, and in the end it is a personal decision that each family must make for themselves.

The inquest

Although for many people, the funeral is a statement of finality, those parents who have to be subjected to an inquest must remain in a state of limbo, perhaps for weeks afterwards, until the inquest has taken place, thus preventing them from beginning the slow and painful journey of recovery.

In the case of Lynne and Paul an inquest was held a few weeks after the death, and two other sets of bereaved parents attended as well as them. The inquest took place in a court room and the Coroner, a police officer and a person taking notes were present as well as the six parents. Lynne found the inquest extremely painful, particularly as she had to take the stand, as was the policy of that court.

It brought it all back again. We'd had the funeral and everything seemed to be finished; and then they started it all over again with the inquest. I felt it was cruel and completely unnecessary; it didn't prove anything.

A direct consequence of the inquest and an additional source of pain was that a report of the death appeared in the local newspaper. Despite the fact that it said that the baby had died of natural causes and that the parents were in no way to blame, Lynne felt that even that denial put emphasis on the *possibility* of the parents being in some way to blame and she was upset by this report.

At the inquest held on Marian's baby, the Coroner also had several cot death parents together, in order that each set of parents could gain support from each other. Nevertheless, this had the effect of delaying the inquest until about six weeks after the death of Marian's baby since it was the policy of the Coroner to wait until there were three sets of cot death parents before holding an inquest. The inquest was therefore 'hanging over' Marian, particularly because she was not officially informed of the post-mortem findings until after the inquest. (Nevertheless, a police officer had rung her a few days after the baby's death to reassure her that the death had been caused by a virus.)

Marian was put on the stand first, in the hope that, as a nurse, she might be able to help the other parents. She was asked whether, with her medical knowledge, she had understood what had happened at the time of the death (that it was a cot death). She replied that she just felt guilty and thought that it was her fault (because the baby died whilst in the car, on a short trip out). Her words then became the headline in the local press, and once again caused needless additional distress.

The inquest seems to be a cruel additional burden placed upon the bereaved parents, and when it is carried out simply because it happens to be the practice of that particular area (as in the above cases) and is merely verifying the post-mortem findings, an unnecessary and pointless exercise. Fortunately, fewer areas now are carrying out this automatic practice.

3 Receiving support

Ideally, as soon as possible, the hospital should alert the GP and make available their paediatrician. The GP should call on the couple and should also inform his Health Visitor, so that she can continue to make regular calls.

The 'primary care team': doctor and health visitor

In my own case, though my own doctor was on holiday, a member of his team, well known to me, called round on the day after the death, and the Health Visitor too called on the same day. After that, however, I had no further contact with the surgery until some weeks later, when the eruption of a rash caused me to ring for an appointment. My doctor chose to come to me instead, and this gave me the opportunity for a long and reassuring conversation with him. However, I think I would have appreciated still more organized medical support. In this respect, time has brought about improved knowledge of cot death and of the needs of bereaved parents and, as a result, in many areas, better support by the doctor/Health Visitor team.

Parents are desperate to relieve their feelings by talking of the death, and if friends are unwilling to be the recipients, it becomes all the more essential for the doctor/Health Visitor team to give this support, and in due course to direct the parents to other counsellors or 'befrienders'.

Dr G. said that at the first interview with the parents after the baby's death, he would make it clear to them that he was available, by telling them, 'Come and see me in a few days, in case there are any problems you want sorted out.' However, he told me that not everyone takes up that offer. I suggested that sometimes people were nervous of wasting the doctor's time, and he repeated that this was the very reason why he gave them this opening.

Lynne's GP had given her just such an invitation, and when she went to the surgery to make an appointment, he called her in straight away, ahead of other people who were waiting, and talked to her for half an hour, which gave her a great deal of reassurance.

Maureen and Rod felt that from their initial reception at the hospital onwards, they had received 'enormous support' from the medical profession generally, including the Primary Care team. The Health Visitor had come the next day; the GP came for a second time, two days later, after they had had the post-mortem result, in order to make sure that they understood what was happening. The midwife came almost daily for about two weeks, and very regularly after that.

On the other hand, Sue and Neville were not happy with their Health Visitor, neither before nor after baby Anthony's death. Sue used to hear from other mothers that on visiting them, the Health Visitor had said, 'Oh, I do hate it when my children die. I must go and see her [Sue].' Sue recalls, 'I used to hear from people all round the area that Mrs Thing (I can't remember her name) had been saying she ought to come and see me, but she never came, she never saw us, so we never had any help from her whatsoever.'

Maureen B. was very upset by the fact that her doctor told her to 'have another baby', when he came to her after the death. This suggestion could not have been more tactless, because only a few weeks before, he had been consulted by her husband, who had just had a vasectomy. She felt he should have remembered this very significant fact and should not have made that comment, which caused her much additional pain. However, in contrast, the Health Visitor was very helpful and in fact came after Michelle's death bringing flowers.

Though the official support comes through the Health Visitor there is sometimes a liaison through her between the community and maternity hospital and, in these circumstances, the midwife is likely to be informed. Midwife, Mrs E., said that sometimes, if a midwife knows a family well, she may wish to visit them, if she feels that such a visit would be appreciated. Maureen A. was told by her midwife that one of the sisters at the hospital where her baby son had been treated for jaundice, was very upset at the death and wanted to come to see her. However, in the end, she did not come and Maureen felt it would have been better if she had said nothing to the midwife, since Maureen was counting on people's reliability a lot more than she would have done normally.

If the professionals seem to be ignoring or rejecting us, it is easy to imagine that this is a sign that they blame us for the death. However, very often the opposite may be true. Dr G. pointed out that it was quite likely that the child had been seen by the doctor within the previous few days for some trivial illness, and the doctor would now wonder if he had missed something and would feel guilty himself.

Sue became aware for the first time, some years after Anthony's death, when she addressed a meeting of Health Visitors, how much hurt and guilt they feel at such a death. I think we have to realize that the professionals are human, that they too may experience a whole range of emotions at the death of one of their patients. Unfortunately, in addition, some may be tactless, thoughtless or quite hurtful in their dealings with the bereaved parents.

Support from other sources

Some parents may seek comfort or help from their religious adviser, as did Lynne. Maureen B. too wanted reassurance from her priest about the fact that baby Michelle had not been baptized.

Many of the officials that the parents meet in the early days, from the medical team, the police or the Coroner, or indeed the funeral director or religious adviser, now have information available about cot death, and any one of them may put parents in contact with the main organization concerned with cot death, the Foundation for the Study of Infant Deaths.

The Foundation for the Study of Infant Deaths

The Foundation is a registered charity, which briefly:

1 raises funds for research into the causes and prevention of cot death
2 gives personal support to bereaved families by letter and telephone and by providing them with leaflets, and also puts parents in touch with 'Friends of the Foundation' groups and other bereaved parents, who will act as 'befrienders'
3 acts as a centre of information about cot death, providing literature for parents and professionals, and caters for the exchange of knowledge within the UK and abroad

How can contact with the Foundation or other bereaved parents help?

Parents may telephone the Foundation direct, to talk about their feelings and to seek explanation and advice. The Foundation have available on their staff, informed and experienced people who listen with sympathy and understanding to anyone who wishes to telephone. In addition, those parents who prefer to write to the Foundation will receive a personal reply giving answers and explanations to specific questions and worries. They will also be sent the latest newsletter and an invitation to complete the Foundation's questionnaire, if they wish. (In this respect, I regret that no such questionnaire was available to be completed when Amanda died, since I should have liked to have felt that her death was contributing to further knowledge of the subject.) A paediatrician is also available at the Foundation office on certain days, to answer further questions.

Often, other members of the family and friends may contact the Foundation in order to be reassured, or to gain greater understanding. Health Visitors and GPs too are also grateful for additional support when a cot death occurs in one of the families they are visiting. Bereaved foster parents, adoptive parents and child minders may also contact the Foundation.

As well as giving personal support, the Foundation produces various leaflets intended to explain what is known about cot death, the diverse feelings experienced by bereaved parents, and the research that is going on in different areas which is funded by the Foundation. It also gives advice or counselling about the next baby. Initially, the parents may only need the reassurance that their feelings of anger, grief, bitterness or guilt are similar to those of other cot death parents. If they then wish to have a direct contact with other parents to discuss their feelings, the Foundation may know of a local person who will have reached the stage when they can offer this support. (Sometimes, the reverse situation occurs. A doctor or Health Visitor may be able to refer the parents to another bereaved family, and that family may give the newly bereaved parents information about the Foundation.)

Outsiders may sometimes feel doubtful about the benefits to the bereaved family of becoming involved with the Foundation, or its parent groups. Even the parents' own parents may believe that the young couple should be 'putting the tragedy behind them' and thinking of the future. However, there is no doubt in my mind that the availability of information on cot death is of supreme importance, and that the ability to discuss the tragedy with others is a big step in the healing process that must eventually take place.

Ignorance of the nature of cot death can only add to the confused emotions, particularly guilt, that are felt, whereas knowledge not only clarifies the situation and helps remove some of the self-doubt, but also enables the parents to give better information to their families, friends and neighbours to help them to understand and to dispel any unfounded suspicion.

Seeking help

Parents do not necessarily seek help immediately, though I was told that some parents have rung the Foundation within hours or days of their babies' deaths. Some parents make contact at a later date, for the first time, and many continue to seek help from the Foundation, over a long period, when there is a crisis, when they are upset, if they want advice on pregnancy or a subsequent baby or if they just want to chat. They can, if they wish, be put on the Foundation's mailing list and will then continue to receive information about cot death via the newsletters.

Sue and Neville, when they ran a support group, found that parents often contacted them, for the first time, six to eight weeks after the death of their baby, perhaps partly because both the automatic support from health professionals and the support from friends and family seemed to abate at around that time.

Alternatively, in their initial state of shock, parents may not know what they want to do, but after some weeks find that their need to be in contact with people who have had the same experience as themselves has grown rather than diminished, and at this stage, they are very glad they have the information at hand.

In my own case, there was very little information available at the time of Amanda's death, and it was only when four or five weeks had passed and I began to feel stronger, that I had a positive *need* to know more about the mysterious illness that had caused the death of my daughter. It was only by chance that I discovered an organization called the British Guild for Sudden Infant Death Study, which was conceived at around the same time as the Foundation and was later absorbed by it. I communicated by letter with Dr Bernard Knight (now Professor Knight) who, with his wife Jean, was the founder of the British Guild, and he subsequently referred me to the Foundation.

During the first few weeks before I knew of the existence of any support groups, I had felt extremely isolated, and once I was aware of their existence, I realized how important such organizations were to a bereaved person. The Foundation, which had only come into being about a year before, was not then as organized as it is today in putting bereaved parents in contact with one another. Nevertheless, for me the written word was sufficient, the literature from both organizations extremely helpful and the personal letters from Professor Knight very comforting.

At the time of their baby's death, a few years later, Sue and Neville received information about the Foundation at a much earlier stage than I did. They were told about it by the Registrar and were given a leaflet and a newsletter. They made contact with the Foundation about a week later. However, there was no local parent for them to contact. (They were able to get in touch with the parents of a child who had died of meningitis, but the situation was not the same.) Though their friends sat with them and let them talk, no one knew what they were feeling. Sue wished that they had been able to make contact with other local cot death parents at that time. Nevertheless, the existence of the Foundation was helpful to Sue. When she felt 'low', she would telephone the Secretary of the Foundation and sometimes would receive a telephone call from her.

Lynne was given a list of various organizations from her rector, and he included the address of a local 'befriender', who had contact with other bereaved parents. She did not, however, make contact with him for some weeks – not, in fact, until after the inquest had taken place. By this time, she had ceased to see so much of her local friends, who had supported her initially, and she started to feel very empty. It was at this stage that she felt in need of some assistance.

She found the 'befriender' very helpful and talked to him for some time; he gave her the name of another parent who lived nearby and she met and talked to the other mother on a few occasions. Subsequently, she was introduced by this mother into a group that existed in that area. Members would mention bereaved parents that they had been in contact with and report on any visits that they had carried out. New parents were encouraged to talk of their experiences. Lynne found this helpful and did not find it necessary to go back to any of the professionals for further help.

Maureen A. did not know of the Foundation's existence, prior to Timothy's death. She received a leaflet from one of the official sources, as well as being given the telephone number of the Compassionate Friends. However, after her initial contact with both organizations, she felt that the former was more suited to her needs. She would have been very isolated without the Foundation, because, unlike some, she received very little support from friends.

Jane and David were given information about the Foundation and a 'befriender' at their first meeting with the paediatrician, and they were able to meet the befriender later that day. Because of their immediate contact with the Foundation, Jane did not experience the isolation felt by parents who had lost their babies at a time when information and help were more sparse.

Maureen B. received a Foundation leaflet from her doctor. However, she did not make contact with them herself. On one occasion, whilst at the local nursery school, where her children attended, she was in rather a distraught state, and had to explain to the headmistress what had happened. She, by chance, was able to put Maureen in touch with another bereaved mother who, as well as 'befriending' her, also arranged for the Foundation to contact her. She found it helpful knowing that other people had had the same experience as herself, and benefited from being able to talk to someone else. After the first contact was made, the Foundation rang and talked to her, and it was left that she would ring them if she needed further help.

Twins and Multiple Births Assocation

Parents of twins may already know of the above association and may have been a member of a Twins Club from the time that they knew that twins were expected. They may need specific help with the loss of a twin, as well as the other support they receive. They may wish to retain membership of their Twins Club and to stay in contact with the parents of other twins, who may have particular understanding of their loss. They can also send for leaflets on the death of a twin and be introduced by TAMBA to parents who have suffered a similar loss.

'Friends of the Foundation' groups

Some areas have local groups of 'Friends of The Foundation', like the one Lynne attended, some of which are structured organizations and some more casual, in which parents make themselves available to newly bereaved parents in order to give counsel or 'befriend' them. Some local organizations have an arrangement with doctors or hospitals and are informed of any new cases of cot death, so that they can make an immediate approach to the parents. Others look out for reports in local papers, in order to be able to offer their help.

I attended at a coffee morning with a group of bereaved mothers. The group was an assortment, ranging from the 'senior' mother and hostess, Pam, whose baby had died fifteen years before, to others whose babies had died during the past four or five years and more recently. Two of the group were pregnant; two mothers had not become pregnant since the deaths of their respective babies and there was a variety of toddlers and under-fives, some of whom had been born after the death of their siblings.

The group was supportive and encouraging to those mothers who wanted another child, or who were approaching the birth of one. They mentioned news of other absent parents, and newly bereaved parents who wished to be put in touch with others. One or two of the group were contemplating reversals of sterilization operations or had recently had them carried out. They also talked of minor fund-raising projects, but these were not the main focus of the occasion.

Because the mothers at the meeting were at various 'stages' since the deaths of their babies, they did not necessarily want to talk about the death itself, and in fact, for much of the time, it could have been a mother and toddler group meeting, with much talk of domestic problems, gardening and children, as well as the topics related to cot death. The very fact that the cot death was not a 'taboo' subject, freed the gathering to talk of many non-related topics, returning to the subject if some particular point occurred to them.

This group had a general policy of trying to link up newly bereaved parents with other parents whose bereavement was more than a year before. In addition, they tried to introduce people who would be comfortable with one another, of similar ages and attitudes. Initially, 'senior' parents would meet the newly bereaved on a one-to-one basis and not at such a large gathering as the one which I attended. Caroline, who had recently arrived from another district, felt that it was helpful to meet another bereaved mother on her own, to talk through the bereavement. Her Health Visitor had been able to put her in touch with another mother, and she had found this a great help. Subsequently, she went with the other mother to a group meeting, where the emphasis was on fund-raising, but she preferred the more casual approach of the group which we were visiting. Mothers may not be ready to be plunged into fund-raising activities at an early stage after bereavement, and such groups, valuable though they are at raising much-needed money for research, cannot substitute for parents who are prepared to be 'befrienders' and to talk and listen to the newly bereaved.

4 Emotions and reactions

A whole range of emotions are experienced by the parents of a cot death victim, most of which they have not felt before, or experienced in such intensity. Mandy described her feelings as 'desolation, sheer disbelief, horror, guilt and even physical pain', and most parents share a spectrum of similar emotions.

One of my first reactions to the tragedy was disbelief that such a thing could be happening to me. Most people tend to regard a tragic event as something that happens to other people and when one occurs in their own life, they find it almost impossible to believe it is really happening. In addition, the suddenness of the cot death plunges the parents into a horrifying situation, which contrasts vividly with the pleasant life they were experiencing only a few hours or even minutes earlier. To me, the discovery of our baby had all the qualities of a nightmare. Similarly, Sue described her feelings as 'disbelieving horror'.

I also remember thinking that I would never be able to put from my mind the sight of my baby, when my husband and I first discovered her. But even when some of the horror had abated, the sadness and emptiness remained, filling the wintry days of the months that followed. For me, the long wait before I could hold my own baby in my arms again, seemed interminable and my loving little boy could not compensate for the lost child.

I cried a great deal, mainly when I was on my own. I felt very bitter that my baby had died without any opportunity to see anything of life and I could see no point in her having been born, if she was only to die so soon. I felt resentful about the year of my life that had been spent in producing and caring for a new baby who had so prematurely been taken from me, feelings shared by Sue, who spoke of a complete year wasted with nothing to show at the end of it. I felt certain that no other death could be so painful for a parent as that of its child. As well as the sadness and the longing to have my baby back, or to be able to return magically to the days before it happened, as I did sometimes in dreams, I was tormented by other feelings – fear and guilt. These are emotions which are perhaps unavoidable, but whereas no one has the right to expect the parents of a dead child to bury their feelings of grief and sadness, it would be beneficial to try to put aside their emotions of fear and guilt.

Vulnerability

The assumption that my own family was in some way 'immune' to tragedy, which perhaps we all feel until it strikes us, caused me to be irrationally afraid when I found that, after all, my loved ones had no special protection. I found that I was quite petrified that my son would die in his sleep without warning, like his sister, and sometimes in the night I even imagined that my husband had stopped breathing. These irrational fears lasted for some months, and I do not know of any way of banishing them. Only the knowledge that others feel the same way, and the passing of time itself, will help them abate.

As soon as the confirmation of death is received, the parents probably begin searching their minds for some clue as to the cause of death, and this probing continues relentlessly during the first weeks, as the parents sift through the events over and over again. The lack of any obvious reason for the death makes us feel even more vulnerable and we seek some logical explanation. We have grown up to expect that the majority of people die of a cause. They die because they are old, or ill, or because they have been involved in some sort of accident. Sudden deaths are almost always more shocking than anticipated deaths, for there is no time to prepare for the departure from our lives of someone we love.

However, if there is an explanation for that death, it lessens our own feelings of vulnerability. If someone we know dies in a car accident, we may drive more slowly for some considerable time; if someone dies of a heart attack, we may justify it to ourselves by recalling that he was overweight or had suffered chest pains. By giving ourselves a reason for these unexpected deaths, we may feel that we have the power to prevent them happening to us, or to those within our care. Because, in the case of a cot death, the cause of the death is not known, it seems that it is not in our power to prevent it happening to anyone else we love. So we search for an explanation, in order to convince ourselves that we are in control of our own destiny again.

Similarly, outsiders are also seeking a reason for our cot death, because the occurrence of an unexplained sudden death makes them feel vulnerable too. This is, no doubt, the reason for some of the suspiciousness felt by some acquaintances who are not intimate enough with the bereaved parents to trust them. By telling themselves that the parents must have been guilty of negligence, or worse, outsiders are then able to convince themselves that no such tragedy will ever occur in their families.

We, in turn, become our own accusers, and this is the source of one of the most powerful and destructive emotions that we experience, often for weeks and months, and sometimes, though to a lesser extent, for the rest of our lives – guilt.

Areas of guilt

Once we imagine that we have found the reason for the cot death, then we immediately feel guilty at our action or lack of it. Later, our feelings of guilt are compounded by the foolish statements of others who know nothing about the condition, by post-mortem reports where a mention is made of respiratory infections or viruses, or such suggestions (which were made more frequently in the past) as inhalation of vomit or suffocation.

Suffocation

One of the very first questions I asked the Coroner's officer when Michael and I were interviewed by him was, 'How can you tell she didn't suffocate?' I asked that in spite of the fact that Amanda had no pillow and that her mattress was bought as a 'safety mattress' made of aerated material.

We do sometimes hear, in media reports about cot death, of apparent 'confessions' by parents to suffocation, and one cannot help wondering how many parents, particularly those with no previous knowledge of cot death, imagine that their baby has suffocated because, at that moment, there seems to be no other logical explanation. Parents who, like me, placed their babies on their stomachs, in their cots, and parents whose babies were on their backs, but were found with blankets over their faces, are quite likely to jump to this incorrect conclusion.

Professor Bernard Knight, in his book *Sudden Death in Infancy* (Faber, 1983), states that it has been found that all fabrics used in the manufacture of bed-coverings, such as woollen blankets, cotton and nylon sheets and other man-made fabrics, easily admit enough air through the weave to allow full respiration for the relatively slight needs of an infant. In addition, other tests have proved that a healthy baby will lift and turn its head away from obstructions in a search for air.

In my case, I was immediately reassured by the Coroner's officer that marks on the side of Amanda's face indicated that her nose was not obstructed. So the police investigation and the post-mortem examination, which subsequently confirmed that the death was by natural causes, were helpful to me initially, and erased one possible line of guilt or worry. However, the relief I felt on hearing this verdict was short-term, for it opened a new avenue of guilt, by suggesting that 'acute respiratory infection' was a factor in the baby's death.

The common cold

Amanda had had a cold, which caused her one very bad night. For some reason, perhaps because I had no transport available the next day to take her to the doctor a mile away, I merely sought advice from the Health Visitor on the telephone. I was then satisfied that provided she continued taking her feeds without difficulty, there was nothing much to worry about. The next day, she was much better and a full three days passed in which she appeared to have recovered completely, before her death occurred.

When I was asked if she had been ill, and reported that she had had a cold, I was amazed to find that it was assumed that there was a link between that and her death. But once the verdict was pronounced, the significance, in my mind, of the cold grew, so that it seemed, with hindsight, unbelievably foolish that I had not rushed her to the surgery, or insisted that the doctor call to see her. Throughout the months that followed, that was my particular area of guilt. However, the likelihood is that if I had taken her to the doctor, the subsequent events would have remained unchanged, and I would have found something different to feel guilty about.

Jane's baby had had a cold and had been taken to the doctor about ten days before. He had given Jane some medicine to help Naomi to sleep, and told Jane not to worry as it was just a 'little snuffle'. Nevertheless, she still felt guilty. She could not remember precise details of her treatment of the baby on the day prior to her death. She wondered whether or not she had given Naomi her feed at exactly the right time, or whether it was late.

Maureen B.'s baby, Michelle, had had a cold; Maureen had taken her to the GP and asked for some drops to help her breathe more easily, but he refused saying it was not necessary. Two days later, the baby died. This caused Maureen to feel badly towards the doctor, but it did not diminish her own feelings of guilt about totally different things.

What contribution the cold makes to the child's death is, of course, uncertain and some babies die without such symptoms. Nevertheless, it is important in many parents' minds, so, in order to put it into perspective, I asked doctors their feelings about the significance of the common cold, and what treatment a baby should receive. Dr C. replied:

A baby with snuffles and/or a cough or runny nose, without any signs of throat infection or chest infection or ear infection, probably wouldn't have received any treatment, unless the baby was:
(a) having difficulty breathing through the nose, in which case I might have prescribed drops;
(b) coughing so much that it was keeping itself or the family awake, in which case, I might have prescribed a night-time cough sedative; and
(c) I might have advised aspirin or paracetamol for any feverish episode.

He would not have prescribed antibiotics for a baby with a cold unless there were any other indications that they were required such as the additional infections mentioned above. 'This is the million dollar question, isn't it?,' he commented. 'We don't know if treatment with antibiotics might have made any difference.'

I also asked if he would call to see a baby with a cold and he replied that he would not go out to the baby, unless the mother was worried about something more than just a cold. However, he would have to assess the degree of anxiety of the mother, as well as her personality and her normal behaviour.

I received a similar response from Dr G. when I asked how he would treat a cold.

It is not possible to treat a cold. The only thing you can sometimes do, if the baby has difficulty in feeding, is to give nose drops to dry up the nasal secretions, and I will do that, if it seems to be distressed.

I asked him what he would feel if a cot death occurred to a baby that he had previously seen with a cold.

Both of you are going to be upset at the situation, and both anxious that you made a mistake. The doctor is going to be worried and upset that he's made a mistake in diagnosis and the result will depend on the post-mortem examination. When that comes through and the diagnosis is essentially 'cot death', the doctor at least feels, 'Well I didn't miss meningitis or pneumonia. I'm not guilty of neglect.' It doesn't help the mother very much, but she doesn't have to lose trust in the doctor, who correctly diagnosed an illness which may or may not have contributed to this small child's death. And there's no way, that with present knowledge, we can do anything about that.

Once the post-mortem has established that it was a cot death, there's nothing the mother could have done that would have prevented it, because we don't know what causes it.

This is a very difficult concept for people to understand, because it is assumed that doctors know everything about all diseases, and in fact, there are many illnesses, including those causing deaths, which we do not understand. People are very uncomfortable when we say this – when we say 'I'm sorry, I can do nothing for you. I have no medical treatment that could help you', or 'I have no way of removing your sense of guilt; you feel it because it's natural to feel it.' People have to come to terms with it themselves.

So, in fact, one cannot go on blaming oneself for the lack of a visit to the doctor. Neither can one blame the doctor if such a visit did take place, but there was nothing in the family's medical history to suggest the possibility of a cot death occurring.

I told Dr G. my own feelings that after having a cot death preceded by a cold, I tended to regard a cold in a baby as a very serious thing, whereas, I had not done so before. He replied:

Let me put it into perspective. I reckon to see anywhere between five and ten colds (in people of all age groups) a day. That's five days a week, three hundred odd days a year. In the course of twelve years in general practice, I can only recall two cot deaths.

Colds in babies are a very, very common event. Every child, every baby, will get a cold. You can't then make the jump that the cold causes death. In fact, there is no evidence that the preceding cold led to the cot death. The truthful answer is that we do not know what causes the death; research exists to find out why these babies die. In the meantime, we cannot say that a cold is a serious disease. If we responded with full alarms to every case of cold, we would not save one case of cot death. Because we still can't! So apart from making sure that the child's cold is properly treated, normally there's nothing to be done. The Health Visitor can do that better than the doctor.

Even when studies in certain areas show that particular babies are more 'at risk' because of a number of circumstances, there is still no way that a doctor could forecast in advance that a baby might suffer a cot death. All he can do, even in those particular circumstances is to recommend extra care and perhaps extra alertness when the baby is in contact with any infections. In the circumstances of a baby dying when it does not live in one of those areas where some babies are categorized as 'at risk', or where it was not put into that category in the first place, there is no reason to feel that a visit to the doctor in the days prior to the death would necessarily have changed the course of events.

Inhalation of vomit

Another area of potential guilt is caused by the suggestion that a baby has died as a result of inhalation of vomit. When this verdict was reached by the post-mortem report on Amanda's death (coupled with 'acute respiratory infection'), I was rather shocked and not totally convinced that this could be correct. I had deliberately placed Amanda on her stomach to sleep, having heard rumours of babies choking on vomit, and had always assumed it was safer not to put a baby to sleep on its back. Apart from a little foam around her lips, there was no sign of her having vomited. I was very much reassured by my own doctor telling me that the presence of fluid in the lungs was generally something that was caused at the time of the death, rather than being responsible for the death, for in the no longer functioning body, fluid could move from the stomach to the lungs without hindrance.

This verdict, however, was often used, before the term 'cot death' was put on death certificates and was also responsible for guilty feelings in the parents, since it seemed to imply that they had put to bed a child who subsequently vomited and that they had ignored that child's discomfort.

Sue was another mother who was initially told by her doctor that her baby had inhaled vomit, and she too suffered from guilt as a result of this statement.

Insignificant events

Sue also worried illogically about the fact that she had taken the baby to the allotment on the day of his death and wondered if that visit had been responsible. Lynne did not suffer a great deal of guilt feelings, but she did worry that Andrew might have got too cold after a bath. Mothers often feel guilty about numerous other events preceding the death, such as the bringing up of wind, or the timing or amount of the last feed, none of which have any significance.

Desire for reassurance

Coming to terms with guilt is obviously helped by the reassurance of others. If, as invariably seems to be the case, it is the mother who carries this burden, then the first person to whom she will turn is her husband or partner.

The husband, who may be able to look at the situation in a more detached manner and will not in any way blame his wife for the baby's death, may be surprised at her need for reassurance of this fact. But she may need to be told more than once that he believes in her ability as a mother.

On the other hand, there are marriages in which the husband does *not* believe in his wife or trust her. Such marriages may eventually break down as a direct or indirect result of a cot death, or the breakdown might be avoided by counselling, if this took place early enough. If their problems were caused purely by the cot death, the husband's and wife's faith in each other could perhaps be restored if they received early help, support and information from the medical team with which they were in contact and/or the Foundation. Then, as a team, it would become easier to face the doubts of the rest of the world.

I remember expressing my own self-doubts to my husband over and over again, and he always reassured me, telling me that I was a good mother. I looked to him to be my judge, and just as I assumed that his sadness at the tragedy could not equal my own, so I also assumed that the responsibility for the child (at that age) was mine in total, and if there was any fault, that was mine too.

Even with the knowledge that my husband believed in me, I still felt desperately in need of reassurance from others. During the early weeks, I was a passive being, wanting only to receive, to a varying extent, affection, comfort and reassurance from everyone I knew – acquaintances, advisers, as well as friends and relations. At around this time, I wrote to the Sister of the small maternity unit where Amanda was born. I thought that it was unlikely she would have been notified by any official and I knew I would find it extremely upsetting to explain to her what had happened if I returned in the course of any subsequent pregnancy. However, in particular, I wanted her reassurance too. Foolishly perhaps, I felt that Amanda had come out of the care of her unit into my care and that I had failed her. I half felt that she would write back telling me just that, confirming my own belief in my inadaquacy, and it was a relief to me when she wrote a kind and comforting reply.

I had not realized before how comforting it was to receive

letters of condolence, invariably written with so much difficulty, and I welcomed such letters from friends and relatives who were not near enough to visit me, and read and reread them avidly. Maureen, however, was upset by letters from religious friends saying that she and her baby would meet in an after-life, where there would be no pain. This was no comfort to her; she wanted her baby there and then.

Escape

Once the initial few days have passed, there is a desire to escape from the situation that has been such a traumatic experience. That desire can take a mental or a physical form.

For those people who have been used to escaping into a fantasy world through books and plays, it is possible to distract oneself briefly by listening to the radio or watching the television, though this form of escapism is probably more useful at a later time, because many people find it is difficult to concentrate at first.

A mental escape – if it takes the form of the use of drugs or alcohol to dull the mind – cannot be a good idea. I have already stated various views on tranquillizers and certainly no one can suppose that it would be beneficial to drink so much alcohol as to be oblivious to the pain of the loss. Under such circumstances, alcohol, too, is a dangerous drug.

However, some families, my own included, felt that a physical escape, in the form of a holiday, was not a bad idea. In our case, since our daughter was born in August, we had not had a holiday for a year. In addition, since I was quite convinced that I had to have another baby as soon as possible, it was likely that we would forgo a holiday the following year. (I had a tendency to miscarry and, for that reason, was reluctant to be far from home during pregnancy.) In addition, Amanda had shared our bedroom. Unlike parents whose baby had had a room of its own we could not close the door on a separate room for a few weeks to blot out some of the pain. The empty space at the side of our bed was a nightly torture, from which I strongly desired to escape.

We actually called in at a travel agent on the day of the identification. My husband Michael is someone who deals with such things straight away. I remember thinking that if anyone I knew were to see us, they would wonder how we could possibly be concerned with holidays on such a day. But outsiders could not be aware of the strength of the desire to escape from the horrifying situation. In fact, we were completely indiscriminate and booked whatever was available in a warm place.

The holiday was for me a pause to gain strength, and for the time being, a suspension of reality. However, during the two weeks we were away, I was not able to carry out the necessary mourning, and as the holiday neared its end, I began to feel fearful at the prospect of returning to the reality which I knew I would face at home. Fortunately, the majority of us are unable to escape *permanently* in this fashion, for if we were able to, we would be as damaged as if we had used drugs or alcohol to effect our escape.

However, as a short temporary event, it may be useful, if it can be afforded, for the parents and any remaining children to be together and in a position where someone else is responsible for cooking and cleaning for a few days or more.

Maureen and Rod, whose baby died in December, had been planning to stay at home by themselves for Christmas, the first time they had done this for some years. They had thought it would be ideal, just themselves and the two children. In the event, they could not face being at home for Christmas and Maureen's father gave them money for a holiday in Spain. It was a help while they were there, but Maureen found it hard coming back. However, they were in a hotel, had a lot of good food and, for Nicholas, it was a holiday by the beach with presents, though perhaps not quite like a usual Christmas.

Maureen B. and her husband Tony also went away for a short break. She thought it was helpful, though she felt as if she was in a dream.

However, Jane and David decided against taking a holiday, though people tried to persuade them to do so. Jane regarded a holiday very much as she had regarded tranquillizers; she did not want to feel temporarily better, only to have to face the situation at its worst later on. However, David took two weeks off work so that he was able to give her support at home.

Some people experience a desire to move out of their house permanently, feeling that they cannot face living there. I felt this for a while, but that feeling abated. I had been very fond of my home and my affectionate feelings for it returned, so that I was very glad we had not made a hurried decision to move away before our feelings of grief were resolved. As in the case of all bereavements, it is not a good idea to rush into a move when you are in an emotional state. You might be leaving supportive friends and neighbours just when you need them most. But, in any case, I believe that you need to be in the place of the death in order to mourn properly, and if in the end you decide to move, it should not be for several months, perhaps even a year or more, during which time you will have faced and worked through many of the emotions following bereavement, and will be able to make a reasoned judgement.

Lynne's and Paul's first instinct was to escape from their home and a year or so later, they did in fact move, since they were still not comfortable in their home. Their feelings on the very day of the baby's death caused them to spend the afternoon wandering around visiting estate agents. This strange activity, perhaps similar to my own visit to the travel agent, would probably be regarded as equally heartless by any outsider, ignorant of the emotions one feels. Parents are often in a period of 'limbo' at this time. The husband is not working, as he would normally be, the wife is not occupied with the baby which has taken up so much of her time, and there is a great emptiness which, for the time being, it is impossible to fill with the trivialities that normally take up much of our lives.

Unless you have an opportunity to explain these emotions to acquaintances, it is unlikely that they will have any understanding of the way you feel. You may, in addition, have to put up with comments, as I did, such as 'Lucky you, going on holiday!' It sounds as if they imagine that a holiday could be some sort of compensation for the loss of a baby. I prefer to believe that people do not really think this, but rather are simply at a loss as to the right thing to say if they have little experience of death. We should not condemn genuinely good-hearted people who say unintentionally hurtful things through ignorance.

Friendships and rifts

If you are lucky you may have around you people with whom you can share your sorrow, and who can listen with sympathy and understanding. Maureen B. who had only recently moved to the area, did not know many people but found that one new friend, whom she had contacted on the morning of the death, was very helpful. Lynne too, received great support from two girl friends, whom she had not known well before. Once Paul went back to work, they did not leave her on her own, but would go back to her house after she had taken her older child to play-school or invite her to be with them for the day, until she eventually felt ready to be on her own.

Jane felt that most of her friends dealt with the death very well, and only very occasionally did a friend cross the road to avoid talking to her. She felt she was very lucky and said:

The one thing you learn from something like this is just how nice people are. And their niceness almost hurts. I think it did me a lot of good, because it didn't allow me to feel sorry for myself for too long. I ended up feeling sorry for them, because they were trying so hard to be nice . . . I felt I had to 'snap out of it' for their benefit.

I was in the position of living on the outskirts of a small village, where I was not very well known, but I did have a few very good and supportive friends who listened to me at great length and with great understanding for many weeks after Amanda's death. The value to me of those friends and the benefits of talking about my emotions cannot be measured, but I feel that they contributed greatly to my recovery.

Sue had a strange reaction from one of her friends – a woman with older children who had had an unexpected new baby. When she met Sue the day after the death, she flung her arms round her and said: 'Oh why, why wasn't it my baby that died? Why was it yours?' At that time, this remark hurt Sue dreadfully; how could she think like that about her child?; but afterwards, Sue thought it was the greatest comfort her friend could give – that it was so unfair.

Other neighbouring friends had had a baby boy a week or so before baby Anthony was born. Sue and Neville's daughter had always played with the daughter of these friends and there was an assumption that their two sons would in time also be companions. After the death, the mother avoided Sue and Neville, and this state of affairs continued for some time – at least two months. However, Neville and the other husband finally resolved the situation by deciding to take both families out together. In addition, the friend's husband picked up his own son and depositied him on Sue's lap. His wife was horrified, but Sue had no feelings of resentment about the other baby.

It must be beneficial if someone who is a little more detached can take action to repair a rift in such a friendship before permanent damage can take place.

Not all rifts are caused by the embarrassment of others. I found that I was quite incapable of talking to one mother, who had had a daughter a few days before the birth of my own. This was not due to either resentment or envy of her baby, but because I was very much aware that in any other circumstances we would have been comparing the development of the two babies. Years later, when I knew her slightly better, I was able to apologize to her for my avoidance of her at that time.

Nevertheless, some parents may experience unpleasant feelings of resentment towards others. It is sometimes difficult

not to feel that people who have had a full and happy life
should have died rather than a tiny baby who had no life at all.
On the other hand, Maureen A. was sure that her father, who
was over seventy, and another older relation (who was well
over eighty) were more upset than some people of middle age,
because she imagined they felt they should have died, rather
than the baby.

Mothers may also feel resentful towards pregnant women and
other mothers of new babies. They may also be unable to face
contact with other people's babies.

Reaction to other babies

Sue found that other mothers were concerned that she was
going to be upset by the presence of other people's babies and
would warn her in advance: 'We're having a coffee morning; so
and so's going to bring her baby; do you mind?' However, Sue
said that this never worried her.

Jane imagined that a lot of bereaved mothers did not want
anything to do with other people's babies, but she did not feel
that way; she wanted to be with other babies and spent a lot of
time with a close friend who had a new baby.

I was not resentful of other babies, but I was rather unfair to
one friend who was expecting her first baby, by making her the
recipient of my sad outpourings. I did not realize then the
burden of fear I was placing on her. I now feel that both the
expectant and the new mother deserve consideration from the
bereaved mother, for even the knowledge of a cot death in their
circle of friends may cast a shadow over the delight in their
own new baby and substitute fear for pleasure.

Negative reactions from friends and acquaintances

Mistakes are often made by friends and acquaintances around
you, often good and affectionate people who are trying to do
their best for you. For example, they may make unintentionally
hurtful comments, with the object of cheering you up. Some
may believe that they must be an instrument of distraction and
are likely to change the subject if parents try to speak of the
death. Some, who may be brave enough to bring up the subject,
are concerned if they cause tears. They then feel that they
should not have spoken of the death, since it has caused the
parents pain. They do not realize that, initially at least, the pain
is there constantly, and that tears are only an outward

expression of that pain or grief. Others attempt to offer
consolation, saying for example that the baby may have had a
congenital abnormality or may have continued to be frail had it
survived. They do not realize that such possibilities make no
difference at all to the bereaved person, and are no consolation.
There are also some people who make no acknowledgement at
all of the baby's death, and this is probably most hard to bear.

Death – the unmentionable subject

When infectious diseases, now largely brought under control by
improved living standards, innoculation and the use of
antibiotics, caused the deaths of many people and children in
the community, most families were equally experienced at
comforting each other at such times. However, since people in
the Western world have become more healthy generally, and
premature deaths have become more and more of a rarity, such
deaths have become an unacceptable subject to speak about,
although there has recently been an improvement in these
attitudes. Despite this improvement, deaths which appear to be
inappropriate, for example of children, are still very difficult for
observers to refer to, and this lack of comment often causes
misery and great bitterness amongst the bereaved. What most
parents want is an acknowledgement of their baby's death –
perhaps with an expression of sympathy, because in their
inability to speak of the baby's death, acquaintances deny
parents the right to speak of the baby's life.

It seems to me now that to offer one's sympathy to a
bereaved person is the obvious thing to do, either by letter or
by a personal approach. However, many people are unsure how
to approach a bereaved person; sometimes they take the
coward's way out and ignore them; sometimes they act as if
nothing has happened. The absence of such acknowledgement
creates tension so that normal conversation is difficult, and it
sets up a barrier, which it is very difficult ever to remove.

Mandy wrote to me:

Close neighbours were very supportive, but I did find that several
acquaintances crossed the road as I approached them. In retrospect, I
suppose that they were embarrassed and did not know what to say to
me but, unfortunately, at the time I felt that they were suspicious of the
circumstances in which Sophie died, and that hurt me very much. I did
feel that I was the subject of gossip for a while, but that may have been
my own feelings of guilt and vulnerability.

Maureen A. said that she felt very irritated by the reaction of family, to some extent, but more particularly of neighbours, who preferred to cross over the road or 'look through her' because they were embarrassed themselves.

I really tried to tolerate their point of view, but ended up feeling very angry, thinking, 'Well, I've lost my baby, but they want me to put up with their silly embarrassment.'

Somehow, that's something I still can't put out of my mind. With some of the neighbours, I can never feel completely at ease. One or two of them obviously found it difficult simply to say, 'I'm very sorry about what's happened' – and it didn't need any more than that. Some of them never said anything; it was as though they tried to sweep it under the carpet. Others had to be in a position where they listened to me saying a great deal, even if they didn't say much, but obviously hated the whole idea, and some just preferred that even if I smiled and said 'Hello', they'd look through me; that was very hard.

It certainly seems hard that those most in need of support and reassurance should have to make allowances for others. However, if we are honest, many of us will admit that we were equally incompetent at saying or doing the right thing when confronted with a similar situation, before we had an experience of bereavement.

Suspicion

There are, of course, groups of people who regard the situation of cot death with suspicion. They hear of the sudden death; if they are neighbours, they might see the police arrive. With their lack of knowledge, they jump to incorrect conclusions. The parents may not be able to do anything in this situation; they may be unsure what is being said behind their backs. However, if they are aware of the suspicion or lack of understanding amongst people with whom they are on speaking terms, it might be very helpful to let them see the Foundation literature.

Good and bad has come out of the much increased publicity about cot deaths. Many people are far more knowledgeable now about cot death than in the past. More people than you would imagine have known a case in their own extended family, which is now more likely to be mentioned. Though there has been a backlash of distorted reporting and banner headlines in recent years, this can be counteracted to a certain extent by having information available and being able to put people right with confidence.

My own view is that if you are prepared to stand up for yourself and give informed facts about cot deaths, people will cease to regard you with suspicion. This strength and confidence, unfortunately, may not be forthcoming for several months, and you may be surrounded by doubters in the early weeks, when you are at your most vulnerable and when you most need people's support. However, if you are in a position to put them in the picture, do so, and you may then win that support and sympathy. Remember, you have done nothing to be ashamed of!

Lynne was one mother who felt that local acquaintances were whispering about her. Some time after the baby's death, she found that other children were saying unpleasant things to her son, which she felt must have come from their parents. She felt that people's suspicions had been aroused by the presence of the police and the ambulance. It seemed that the local people did not know the full story, and once Lynne and Paul were aware of the problem, Paul made a point of explaining to them what had happened.

Assumptions of negligence

Some friends, while not thinking that any deliberate action has taken place, may still think you guilty of negligence. Maureen B. found herself on the receiving end of hurtful questions such as: 'Did you bring up the wind before you put her to bed?'

It is difficult to counter such comments when you are insecure and guilt-ridden yourself, and indeed repeatedly asking yourself the same questions. Once again, the assurances contained in the Foundation literature may be sufficient to convince friends that such trivialities are quite irrelevant to the cot death, and would not have altered the course of events.

5 Facing up to the death – carrying on with life

This chapter heading may appear to be a contradiction in terms, but I do not think normal life can satisfactorily be resumed without facing up to the fact that a tragedy has occurred in the family and that the pain of the tragedy will continue for some time. However, I am not suggesting that the bereaved parents should do nothing but think about the tragedy, without respite – the fact is that initially you cannot think of anything else, and if you are distracted by something outside yourself for seconds or minutes in a day, that is a relief.

There may be a period of limbo which lasts until the funeral; it may extend over any holiday or 'break' that the couple takes, away from the normal routine. If an inquest has to take place, then, to a certain extent, any progress that the parents begin to make may be arrested by that ordeal, and their uphill journey may have to begin again. Hard though it must be, if the inquest is not to take place for several weeks, then it would be better to try to put thoughts of it to one side.

When all these events which, in a way, delay the completion of the tragedy, have taken place, the threads of life must be picked up once again. If the husband returns to work, he may find that the necessity to concentrate on his job provides him with a partial relief from the situation. However, the mother's job in many cases may already have been the care of the home and of another child or children. With the arrival of the new baby, her time would have been adjusted to take account of this new member of the family, and therefore the gap in her life would now be accentuated. In addition, many of the household tasks can be carried out in an automatic way, leaving her mind free to think of her sorrow. Nevertheless, an important part of recovery is returning to a routine and even if, for the first two or three weeks, it seems impossible to cope with the burdens of everyday life, sooner rather than later, the mother too must return to the tasks she used to do.

I do not think that at the very early stages it is possible for a shocked, bereaved person to do anything that is very demanding. However, I think that the ritual of performing small tasks has a very important place in our lives at times of crisis. It provides a framework to lean back upon and to build upon gradually. For example, people imprisoned during wartime tried to retain their sanity and self-respect by clinging to the rituals of washing and combing their hair, when minute portions of soap were almost unattainable treasures and a 'comb' might have been a nail. Similarly, the bereaved parent, probably particularly the mother, should get up, wash and dress – and make beds, cook food and wash clothes, or whatever has been the practice of her home, though these tasks at first seem a heavy burden.

I was never a lover of housework, but I found that carrying out the routine household tasks, which I had neglected during the latter months of pregnancy and the two months of Amanda's life, provided a soothing ritual in my life. The fàct that these jobs did not require too much thought meant that I had to find a distraction from the torturing thoughts that would undoubtedly fill my mind, if I allowed them to. I took to listening to the radio a great deal of the time, and although at first my mind wandered and returned to thoughts of my daughter, occasionally I was totally distracted; naturally, the periods of distraction did last longer as time went on.

For the bereaved mother who has no other child to occupy her, it is perhaps even more difficult. She is not likely to be strong enough immediately after the tragedy to seek another job, and after the anticipation of her first child, the empty home will perhaps be even more devastating to her than to the mother who has another child or children to fill it. Jane commented:

The whole circumstances are harder to take if it's your first, because if you have got a surviving child, your life – your day-to-day practical life – changes very little. You are still a housewife and a mother, or a part-time working mother, or whatever you were, but you've still got a child at home. Whereas if it's your first child you've made great preparations for this longed-for first baby. It has appeared, and you are still beginning, in a way, to play at being a mother. Then, all of a sudden, it's taken away from you and in some cases, people are trapped at home, with no children at all.

For those mothers who are able, a return to their original job may be helpful, though that too may have some pitfalls. Jane was fortunate enough to be able to return to her former employer.

My boss who I had worked for before I had Naomi created a job he didn't really have, for me to go back to. So I just went back to work in the same place, and I went back after two weeks, the same day as David. I only worked part time, but it was amongst people I knew.

She was appreciative of the fact that her boss was paying her for something he could have done himself, or got someone else to do. It was helpful to her to be able to go back to a job where, because it was a small firm, everyone was familiar to her and knew about the baby. However, there were occasional unavoidable moments of embarrassment. These were usually caused by brushes with people she knew slightly, who were surprised to find her back at work, but who did not know that the baby had died. One occasion which was particularly embarrassing was when a member of the staff who knew of the baby's death, tried to stop another occasional caller who did not know, from making a flippant comment like 'Have you got fed up with the baby already?' Bad though that was, the attempt to usher him swiftly from the room, in order to save Jane's feelings, caused even more mutual embarrassment, lasting for months after. In such circumstances, Jane felt it would have been better to let her tell for herself what had happened, and then make some attempt to put the visitor at his ease.

I experienced one or two embarrassing moments of this kind, one particularly upsetting one when an acquaintance rushed up to me in a shop and asked me, 'What did you have? A boy or girl?' I answered with the truth as calmly as I could and she, no doubt at that moment as shaken as I was, simply turned away. However, on the other occasions when such a thing happened, the recipients of the news, though shocked, did try to express their sympathy.

Jane had tried to inform acquaintances and friends, but felt there were bound to be people that you would miss. Neville, when he returned to work, was helped by the fact that his employers had already notified some of his customers of the death of his son.

There were some people I made a point of writing to, when I was able to tackle this task, about a month or two after the baby's death. These were acquaintances with whom I might come into contact only rarely, but whom we would not have automatically telephoned in the days immediately afterwards.

Seeking help

It is around this time, or perhaps two or three months after the death, that the passivity which I mentioned earlier is replaced by a more positive attitude. In my own case, it meant I sought out a magazine, in which I remembered seeing a letter about the sudden death of a baby, and made an effort to find out about the support group which was mentioned in it: the British Guild for Sudden Infant Death Study.

Mandy, feeling isolated after her baby's death, wrote to the newspaper *Reveille*, asking if other mothers who had shared the same experience would write to her. At that time in 1976, out of about fifty letters she received from cot death mothers, only four knew of the existence of the Foundation.

Mandy, who like me gained relief from writing, explained why she had written her letter.

Probably my main reason for writing to *Reveille* was a yearning to write everything down on paper to get it out of my system, as it were, and also for support and reassurance from other parents. I received about a hundred letters, from bereaved parents of many kinds and also a wide range of ages, their children being from stillborn to forty-five years of age, ninety-nine per cent beautiful but sad. These gave me comfort and I felt very sorry for these other parents, who enabled me to realize that I was not alone in my grief. In retrospect, I am glad I did write that letter, because it was very beneficial in my coming to terms with my situation.

It may be at about this time that parents who have already been given information about the Foundation, or any other support groups, make a point of getting in touch with them. As previously stated, not everyone seeks help from the Foundation or from a befriender immediately. Some people want to mourn quietly and privately, speaking exclusively to intimate friends or understanding relatives. But after some time, they too may reach a point, as I did, when they must seek more experienced help, or when they feel they want to understand more about their baby's death. This realization of the need for help is, in my view, a very positive action at whatever stage it occurs, and is perhaps one of the most important steps towards recovery.

The baby's possessions

Sooner or later, parents have to make a decision about the baby's possessions. It is surprising how difficult it often is to decide what is to happen to the clothes, the pram and other baby equipment, perhaps because the eventual decision about those items may be inextricably connected to thoughts of future children, which, of course, involves a much greater decision.

In my own case, I dealt with the nappies and other clothes very quickly – even before my holiday – washing, ironing and airing them, just as I would have done if Amanda had been alive. It was a bitter experience for me, ironing those little clothes with no prospect of a baby wearing them in the near future.

However, only when I later faced the clean, aired clothes, as well as the unworn presents of dresses and playsuits, did I experience real difficulty in knowing what to do with them. There were, in addition, the large items of baby equipment, which on the night of Amanda's death had been hurriedly placed in our spare room by Michael, but which as time went on, presented a sad reminder of the tragedy and made the room an area we were reluctant to use.

Eventually, I packaged the clothes up and put them in a dry linen cupboard. The decision was too big for me to make at that time. I wanted another baby, but I did not know whether I would want that child to use Amanda's clothes; indeed, I could not be sure that I would have a child of the same sex and what, if any, of the clothes would then be suitable to use. It was a decision that I would return to when and if that time came. Eventually, I did have a second daughter, and I got a certain amount of pleasure from her wearing her sister's clothes, which she certainly would have done anyway, had Amanda survived.

The problem of the equipment was resolved for me by another member of my family who borrowed the baby bath and carry-cot. It was the carry-cot which caused me the most soul-searching, partly because it was the only item of equipment which had been bought new for my daughter, and partly because it was the place in which she had died. All the other equipment had been passed around the family and used by several cousins, as well as my son, and I knew I would have no compunctions about eventually using that again. But in any case, I was glad to remove it all from the spare room so that we could reinstate the room to its original use. Eventually, I found that once the carry-cot had been used by another of the continuing line of cousins, I felt able to use it again.

Sue and Neville found, like me, that the room containing the baby equipment became a room they were reluctant to enter, and it was some time before Sue was ready to tackle this. Initially, however, a next-door-neighbour dealt with the bucket of wet nappies which had been left at the end of the day of the baby's death, whilst Neville disposed of the bedding that had been in use.

However, Sue wanted to deal with the remainder of the baby's possessions herself, and about three or four months later, she felt able to do this. On a lovely hot clear day in the summer, feeling better than she had on other days, Sue went to the baby's room which had been virtually sealed up till that time. She packed Anthony's clothes away, painted the walls white, which had previously been decorated with a nursery paper, and she put the cot away. She deliberately left the door and windows open. After that, the room became a spare bedroom again, and they were once again able to use it. Prior to that time, Neville had been very reluctant to go into the room, and did not feel able to decorate it. However, Sue found the work therapeutic.

Like other mothers, Sue kept the baby clothes, but two years later, she gave most of them away to an expectant mother with financial problems, having first explained the situation to her. The rest of the clothes were given to another woman who was fostering a child, whilst the pram was given to a jumble sale. Sue did not have another child herself.

Like Sue, Jane was helped by friends, who came on the night that Naomi died and went round the house and removed everything that had anything to do with Naomi and put it in the nursery – the carry-cot, pram, sterilizer, bottles and so on. The same friends came back a day or so later, and without being asked, and without Jane knowing, went through the clothes that were in the wash and moved them to the nursery too. They offered to come and sort *everything* out, but Jane refused their offer, and after about seven or eight weeks she went into the nursery and sorted things out herself.

She gave the pram and carry-cot to the Health Visitor and asked her to take them away. She threw away some things (bottles, for example), but packed up the clothes in boxes and put them away. Naomi was her first baby and was not very old when she died, so the clothes were hardly worn.

I wasn't sure what I wanted to do. When James was born, because he was a boy and she was a girl, there were very few things he could have worn anyway. Basically, it was white 'babygrows' and vests, and once they all went in together, I couldn't tell which ones had been hers and which had been bought for him.

Once her son was born, Jane gave away the remaining clothes. She felt that she would not consider having another baby for a few years, and she did not want to keep the clothes for that length of time. In any case, once she had had James, she came to the conclusion that if she had had a girl, she would not have wanted to dress her in little outfits that were definitely identifiable as Naomi's. However, at the time of Naomi's death, she was not sure, so she felt she had been right in retaining the clothes and making the final decision later. She felt that if she had given away or thrown away most of Naomi's things at the time of her death, she would have regretted it later.

Maureen B. also retained her daughter Michelle's possessions, until long after her subsequent child, a boy, was born. At the time of her death, Michelle was already in a room of her own, which had been decorated suitably for a daughter. After a time, Maureen redecorated the room, changing the pink paintwork to blue, and put one of her two older sons in there. This was probably a helpful thing to do; it meant that the door could be left open, and once the room was repainted, it was not such an upsetting sight.

Lynne's baby's bedroom had previously been a study, and had not yet become fully a baby's room, so that made it easier to reinstate it to its former use. In addition, her baby did not have many possessions of his own, as a great deal of his things had belonged to his older brother. He had his own nightgown and Lynne took this to the funeral director's for him to be buried in, together with a little toy. His shawl and things that Lynne had bought just for him, she took to the local hospital, and gave them to the children's ward, with some of his toys. She kept some of the unworn clothes that had been given to him; she did not know at that stage whether she would use them if she had another baby, so, like Jane, she delayed making a decision about them, but simply packed them up and put them away.

She dealt with them very quickly and similarly packed up the larger equipment without very much delay. She and her husband Paul worked together. Lynne went through the drawers, and she and Paul packed the cot up together; they boxed the things up and put them in their parents' lofts.

Eventually, when their next baby was born, they changed the carry-cot; they were unwilling to put the new baby in the carry-cot in which Andrew had died. They also bought a new Visivent 'safety' mattress. Lynne decided when she was pregnant, that she would not be able to use the carry-cot again for sleeping purposes (though she would have considered using it only as a pram). She bought a different make of carry-cot, which would nevertheless fit on the old wheels, and sold the old one.

Maureen and Rod's baby had been sleeping in a small bedroom by himself, and the midwife said that for Nicholas' sake, they really ought to take down the cot and put away the clothes as quickly as possible. Rod had a week off work and they carried out the task of putting the things away very quickly – after the funeral, but before Rod returned to work. They just packed everything away, except for a few soft toys which they had already received as Christmas presents for the baby. They took these to a children's ward.

The police had taken away the carry-cot mattress for examination and they did not return it. So Maureen and Rod had to replace that for their subsequent baby, Julie. The baby clothes and so on were mostly those which had either been loaned to Maureen by her sister-in-law, or had originally belonged to Nicholas. When it came to having another baby, there were only about three items of clothing that Maureen did not want Julie to wear. Maureen was not sure whether these were clothes that had belonged solely to Timothy, but in any case, she felt they were very closely connected with how she remembered him at the time that he died. Apart from that, she kept everything and used it again.

Child benefit and other finances

The Child Benefit Order Book states in its yellow pages that you must report to your local Social Security Office any changes, and this includes the death of a child for whom benefit is being claimed. Sometimes the Order Book is returned with the dead baby's name crossed through; this can be very upsetting, so one should ask for a new cover without mention of the baby's name. I had a horror of benefiting from my daughter's death and I sent off my order book as soon as possible for amendment.

After a few weeks, I also dealt with the Premium bonds which were in Amanda's name. These amounted to one or two pounds, hardly worth the bother of withdrawing, and the filling out of the long Post Office form which it was necessary to complete was another ordeal. Nevertheless, it would have been so much worse to receive a letter addressed to her, if by some remote chance the Bond had won a prize. If I could have spoken about it, I would have liked to assure the postmistress that I was not an acquisitive mother, eager to get my hands on the miserable two pounds that had been my daughter's sole estate. It was simply another step in asserting the finality of her death. Nevertheless, when my second daughter was born, I particularly asked relatives not to put any money in her name, and it was not until she was a year old that I opened a Post Office account for her.

Lynne put Andrew's money presents into his older brother's account, with the agreement of the family who had given these presents, while some people like to make a donation of such gifts to the Foundation or another charity.

Photographs

Everyone I spoke to had photographs of their baby, according to the custom of their house – some framed on the wall or mantelpiece, some contained in a family album.

It surprises me now, when I look back and remember, that I actually wondered whether it was right to keep the few photographs I had of Amanda or whether I should throw them away. At that time, I was still in need of reassurance that I was 'allowed' to remember her. Thank goodness, Michael, in a practical manner, said, 'Throw them away! Why should you want to do that? She was a member of our family, wasn't she?' For a few months after Amanda's death I carried the folder containing five photographs around in my handbag. Then, for a while, I put them away in a cupboard, but after my second daughter was born they took their rightful place in the family album.

Another mother once expressed similar doubts to me and by that time, I was quite sure about the answer. Sadly, she was overruled by a relation, who took the photographs from her and destroyed them. Unfortunately, in some cases, parents are still young enough to be regarded as children by their own parents.

Lack of experience of death

Many bereaved parents are likely to be young themselves and thus may not have been faced with the death of someone close before. Even those parents to whom I spoke, who had already lost a parent, found themselves faced with completely different emotions on the loss of a baby, though their experience of death may have armed them to deal with the mechanical problems of arrangements that need to be made.

However, when faced with unfamiliar emotions, many parents are unsure how they should behave. They take their cues from friends and relations, who are also faced with a new situation and who may not necessarily give them the right information.

As I have already said, in the Western world most people are unprepared for the death of a young baby. No one would suggest that a parent's pain, when a child dies, is any the less in an impoverished Third World country, or was in Victorian England, but when the expectations of the parents are less, the shock at the death is less too. Unlike our predecessors of a hundred years ago, the majority of us do not expect to have a dozen or so children of which two or three will die before adulthood. On the contrary, we usually plan to have only two or three children and we invest all our hopes in those children. In addition, we live in an environment in which that is the normal way of thinking. It is the expectation that our children will all survive and be healthy that makes the shock and impact of the death upon us and those around us all the greater. So the improved standard of health in the West has created a society poorly equipped to deal with death (particularly of babies or young children) in its midst.

In this atmosphere, it is very easy for parents to believe they are at fault in grieving for their dead baby and in wanting to remember and to speak of him or her. Alternatively, they may find it hurtful that their friends will adroitly change the subject whenever the death is mentioned.

Paradoxically, whereas initially other people think the death is so horrifying that they feel unable to speak of it, within a month or so they are likely to imagine that the parents are over it, and may be quite surprised, and even impatient, to see signs of sadness. In this respect, the death of a baby is particularly underrated, and outsiders probably believe that parents should get over this death much more quickly than they would expect people to recover from other bereavements.

Sue and Neville, from their experience of running a support group, felt that parents continued to need support perhaps for as long as a year, to help them through painful anniversaries and birthdays.

I think parents should be reassured that their instinct to mourn and to remember is correct. Nevertheless, we cannot force our emotions on other people and if friends show a great reluctance to discuss the tragedy, it is not our right to inflict our feelings on them. If, on the other hand, we believe that they are changing the subject in order to avoid giving us extra pain, we could reassure them of the helpfulness of being able to express our feelings.

However, if it is impossible to speak of our feelings, I think we have to ask ourselves if we want to continue our friendship with them, or resume it at some future date. If, as is possible,

they are not really good friends, but perhaps parents of our
children's friends or merely neighbours, for the sake of future
good relations, I would accept them as they are and keep up a
masquerade in their presence.

I achieved quite an accomplished act of normality with many
people after the first month or so had passed, though I never
had to do this for my true friends. In that, I was fortunate, for I
was guilty myself of badly letting down a close friend when she
had a bereavement, before my own experience gave me new
insight on the needs of the bereaved.

It is rarely possible at that low and vulnerable time in one's
life to re-educate one's friends, though one may try to do so at
a much later stage. Quite possibly as the tragedy becomes more
distant, so some friends will be a little less embarrassed to
speak of the death, or the parents themselves will become
bolder at bringing up the subject and may give an opening to
the friends. I found that when I wrote letters to the press and to
our local village newsletter on the subject of cot death, this
caused people who had not previously mentioned the subject to
me to say something about it, but this was not until several
months after Amanda's death.

Husbands and wives

Conflict may exist between husband and wife who perhaps do
not share the same intensity of feelings, and this fact in itself
may cause difficulties between them. My own belief is that the
younger the baby that has died, the less likely is the husband
to feel the same degree of pain as the wife. I say this with no
condemnation of the husband, but rather in the hope that it will
help both the husband and wife to understand the other's
feelings.

A bereavement is the loss, not necessarily through death, of
someone (or something) precious from our lives, and the pain
is directly related to how much that person has been a part of
our lives. The closeness of the blood tie itself is not the most
relevant factor. People sometimes feel extremely sad at the
death of a well-known personality, whom they feel has become
a part of their lives, and the 'death' of a soap opera character
may, surprisingly, cause even more grief. On the other hand, it
may be extremely difficult to mourn someone of whom you
have been very fond, when they have physically gone out of
your life, long before their death.

Whereas, in the early weeks of a baby's life, its mother is
almost totally bound up with it, the husband, out at work, may

find the baby takes up only a small percentage of his time. In addition, the wife has already had a growing relationship with the unborn baby throughout her pregnancy, from the time she first started adjusting her food and vitamin intake for the baby's benefit, until the time when almost all her thoughts were focused on the imminent arrival of the new baby.

The husband may initially feel he hardly knows the new baby and may not yet experience the same feelings of affection for his child as his wife does. On the death of the baby, the impact upon his life is often considerably less than upon his wife's. So although, in the considerably more rare case of a baby dying in the latter part of its first year of life or even later, the husband is certainly likely to feel as despairing as his wife, in the more frequent cases where babies die at between two and four months old, there may well be a considerable difference in their feelings. This may lead the husband to think that his wife is not making a quick enough recovery, or that she is dwelling on the baby's death too much. On the other hand, it may cause the wife to feel angry that the husband does not share her deep feelings of grief, or resentful that he has been able to resume his life more easily than she can.

Maureen A. felt that her husband's feelings were very different from her own.

We certainly reacted in different ways, and I really do think that I was more upset than he was and I think that now it is Nicholas and myself that carry the long-term scars. I was very, very upset that within a matter of about five weeks, Rod was saying that he didn't even think about Timothy every day, and I thought that was absolutely awful, because I had nothing else to think about all day, and he'd gone back to work.

We've always got on very well and I think that that was probably the time when there was the biggest gap in our understanding. Well, we came out of it all right; there have been others who haven't.

Lynne, on the other hand, felt that Paul was just as upset as she was. Nevertheless, when he went back to his job, he had something else to occupy his mind, whereas for Lynne, there was nothing. She would wake up in the morning, and think, 'What's the point of carrying on?'

Jane said that David found it hard to talk about the death, and that perhaps as a result of talking about it herself, she probably now felt better than he did. She also felt that possibly we, mothers, were a bit unfair to our husbands, and perhaps asked too much of them. 'If you hurt, you turn to the person that you usually turn to when you're hurt, to be comforted and supported.'

Sometimes the baby may be a 'special' baby, in that it is the first-born, or the first boy or girl of the family. Both Tony and Maureen were particularly happy at the birth of their daughter, Michelle, after two sons, and Tony was 'devastated' at her death. This fact, together with Maureen's feelings of guilt contributed to difficulties between them in talking about the death. The fact that Tony had had a vasectomy was an added problem.

However, not all husbands and wives are divided by the experience. Mandy wrote to me:

Regarding my husband's reaction to this, I can only say that we have a deeper understanding between us because of it. We have hit rock bottom together and we have climbed back up together. Some of the cot death parents I know have had marital difficulties because, for example, their grief reactions are different, they cannot support each other, or even speak about it together, or sometimes one lays blame or resentment on the other.

Luckily, my husband reacted similarly to me when Sophie died; we talked, cried and came through it together.

The grandparents

It is hard when the people closest to us cannot understand our needs. However, our own parents are also sometimes reluctant to be the recipients of our grief. It seems to me that there may be a barrier both between husband and wife and between them and their parents, caused by their very closeness. In particular, the husband and the parents of the baby's mother may share similar feelings that they should not allow her to 'upset herself'. I remember that Michael used to be very contrite when a mention by him of our baby brought tears to my eyes, and I had to reassure him that I wanted to talk about her, and that the tears were not an expression of additional pain.

Similarly, once my association with the Foundation for the Study of Infant Deaths had come about, my father would get quite concerned when I brought up the subject of cot death. As time went on I believe he accepted, without real understanding, that this subject was not to be put behind me but, certainly initially, he must have felt that my concern to find out more about cot death was causing me extra sadness.

As far as the doubts of our loved ones are concerned, it seems to me we have two choices. We can either make it clear to our parents and/or close relations that our desire to talk about the dead baby is very important to us and that talking in itself is not causing additional pain, or we can simply put them in the category of people who do not and cannot understand, and not bring up the subject of the baby in their presence.

I think the latter option is a very hard one to choose, particularly in the case of one's parents. I think that one should strive to make them see that there is more pain in being denied the right to speak of one's own baby than in the speaking. If the parents' wish is purely an unselfish desire to spare their children pain, then they will surely eventually come to understand. However, those parents may first have to recognize that their children are adults, and that there is no simple way to remove the hurt, as they perhaps were used to doing when their children were small.

If it is impossible to talk about the death to parents, or wife to husband, or to any friend, contact with the Foundation, and/or a 'befriender' becomes an absolute essential, and can be of enormous benefit.

6 More about the children – and more about guilt

It may seem that while discussing the problems of the bereaved parents, the children have been forgotten. In practice, it is not possible to forget about them, for apart from the normal care that they require, the death will have had an effect upon them too, and this may be reflected in their behaviour. In addition, their parents' attitude to them may also have been affected.

Insecurity

Maureen was aware of Nicholas's feelings of insecurity, though at two years old, he did not understand the situation clearly, but perhaps recognized that something had gone badly wrong in the family. The first time Maureen went out leaving him with Rod, she found that he was rather clinging. She felt he must be wondering if she was coming back. However, this stage did not last long. On the whole, she did not have many problems with him. He did not wet the bed, nor did he behave naughtily. Nevertheless, Maureen did feel Nicholas had shown signs of grief, although he did not have 'expected' symptoms.

The way that Maureen behaved towards Nicholas was also different from how it might otherwise have been.

Although I tried desperately hard not to be too clinging to him myself, I did find it very difficult to play with him for sustained periods; I found it very much easier to take him out and go places and do things, rather than play 'pretend games'. I didn't have enough 'fun' in me.

We did different things; I took him on train rides, or we'd go somewhere, or do some cooking, or something like that, but I did find the time very difficult to fill up, for quite a while.

In addition, Maureen felt that there had been long-term

effects. She said that Nicholas had found it more difficult to relate to other children, when he started school, than he would have done otherwise and that he wasn't ready for the 'rough and tumble' games.

Nicholas has known when it's been his [the baby's] birthday, although I have never really gone out of my way to say 'Timothy would have been this old or that old'. He's now in the last year of first school, and quite a lot of the other children in his class have got younger brothers or sisters who've started school, as Timothy would have done. And Nicholas is absolutely doting on these younger children.

Maureen was sure he appreciated their subsequent baby, Julie, more than he otherwise would have done. However, this did not stop him from seeming to feel that he had missed out in some way.

He has said that it would be nice if he had a brother or sister at school, partly still because he just doesn't relate well enough to the children that he's with. So I think that's very sad; I didn't realize that might happen.

Lynne's son Philip had also had difficulty in settling down at school, which he started just before the next baby arrived. Immediately after the baby's death, Lynne's family all suffered from a desire to get out of the house, and her son Philip was no exception. During the day, he wanted to be out all the time. Like Nicholas, he seemed to feel insecure but his concern lasted much longer, perhaps because he was four at the time of his brother's death. He was particularly worried at night, and his concern seemed to be that his parents too were going to disappear.

When Lynne had had the baby, Philip had been awoken during the middle of the night and taken to his grandparents; now he was aware that the baby had died in the night. His insecurity caused him to get up in the night regularly, to make sure his parents were still there.

Lynne said: 'He used to take ages to get off to sleep. I used to have to stay with him until he got off to sleep, and then he'd wake in the middle of the night.' Initially, the doctor was worried that Philip would have a breakdown, but nevertheless wanted to avoid him being brought to the surgery, instead advising Lynne to try to keep Philip to his normal life as much as she could. He gave him a sedative to help him to sleep. However, it was not until after Philip started school that he stopped waking in the night.

Lynne felt that Philip was still more sensitive than he would otherwise have been and four years after the death of his brother, he was still insecure. He still did not like his parents going out at night, and if Lynne and Paul did go out, they would always have to tell him when they got back.

Sue and Neville's daughter, Tracey, who was two-and-a-half, acted out the tragedy in her own way by announcing that a teddy bear she had had from birth was dead, and was therefore not to come in her bed any longer. The much-loved teddy was not allowed to be given away to a jumble sale or similar, and was retained until the present day, but he was never allowed to sleep with her again. In addition, Tracey told everyone she knew that 'her baby' was dead.

Some time later, however, she had a further reaction, when her father started a new job and was away from Monday to Friday each week. After he had been doing this for about a month, she became more and more restless, waking during the night. Then Neville's job caused him to be away for a particularly long stretch; the problems became more severe and they reached the stage when within an hour of going to bed, Tracey was awake again. She was very tearful and, initially, would not tell Sue why. Finally, one night she said, 'Daddy's dead, dead like the baby; he's not coming back.'

It is not unusual for children to develop fears at around this age, even without having experienced a traumatic event in the preceding months. Sue and Neville dealt with this situation in a way that it is sensible to deal with any fearful child – by developing calming and reliable rituals – so that Tracey was able to recover her confidence.

From then on, whenever Neville was away, provided he was not completely inaccessible, or out of the country, Sue and Tracey would telephone him every night at six o'clock to say 'Goodnight'. In addition, Sue made tear-off calendars, so that Tracey could see quite clearly the passing of each day till her father returned. These rituals continued for six months to a year, and after that time, Tracey became secure enough again to be quite complacent about her father's absence and his return.

Parents' reactions

Sue's initial feelings towards Tracey were ambivalent.

I resented her dependence on me; I resented her – I wasn't left alone to cry when I wanted to cry; I had to go and feed her, get her a drink, take her to play-school, fetch her back, I had to be doing something for her all the time. I resented that. But equally, I'd found her a most tremendous comfort; I'd got her! I still had a child; I'd proved I could do it once, even if I couldn't do it a second time; but I'd got one.

There is always a likelihood that parents may be possessive and excessively protective of their remaining children. Neville thought that this might apply particularly to a single remaining child and possibly, initially, Sue may have had a tendency to be over-protective of Tracey. 'I suppose that's natural. But having said that, you can't be over-protective; you mustn't be. Apart from anything else, it doesn't do the child any good.'

Mandy confirmed her awareness of her own over-protectiveness:

I feel that the sudden loss of my child has left its mark. . . . Even now that Victoria is eleven and Joby is seven-and-a-half, I worry more about them than I would have done. Victoria gets quite annoyed that she cannot play out with friends, unless I can see her. I drive them everywhere that they go and I take and collect them from school. Also I am over-concerned when they are ill, but these are things I have learned to accept. I work for a GP and he is quite used to me popping my children round to him just to be sure their symptoms are merely a 'bug' and nothing more serious.

Maureen B. had tried to explain the death of their sister to her two boys. She felt that the two-year-old did not understand very much about it, but the older boy was upset and subsequently had some bedwetting problems. Maureen's feelings were similar to Sue's. She felt short of patience with the boys, but at the same time, was very glad to have them. They gave her some sort of purpose in life and she imagined it would have been much harder, if she did not have any children.

Because of the possibility of problems concerning your other children it is a good idea to explain to teachers at school or nursery school, or play-group supervisors what has happened, so that they are prepared for any difficulties.

Twins

Even we who have lost our babies can barely imagine the despair of the parents who find both their babies dead in one night. However, the death of one twin is perhaps almost as traumatic and certainly much more underrated. Whether or not she has other older children, the mother may experience the difficulties described above with the surviving twin. Dr Elizabeth M. Bryan, President of the Twins Club Association, describes in her article, 'The Loss of a Twin', how some people around will ignore the death of the one baby and focus all attention on the live baby. Others will tell the mother that she is lucky to be left with one baby. The mother, however, may have mixed feelings for the survivor. Even whilst being grateful for the fact that the child is there, she may be resentful of the tasks she must continue to carry out for him or her. The live baby may irritate, whilst the dead baby becomes idealized. The live baby may even be rejected by parents who find him too painful a reminder of the dead twin.

Counselling

I asked Dr G. what he would recommend if there appeared to be difficulties between parents and children.

I think counselling is probably a good idea in all such cases. Now the form counselling takes, I don't think matters very much. I don't think it matters very much who does it, as long as it is somebody who has some experience of these problems and obviously, sympathy and understanding. I think, in our practice, the most likely person to do counselling is the Health Visitor, who is an experienced nurse, who has encountered baby deaths before and can cope with it herself. That's rather important; it can be such a powerful event that it can render the therapist unable to help, because their own emotions get in the way. And they have to retain that professional detachment. The Health Visitor is probably also well known to the family already, so in that sense, she isn't seen as intrusive, or suggesting that they have mental problems. She's merely their Health Visitor who has come in to support and talk about their problems – and the counselling then follows on naturally from that. That's actually what happens in our practice. In some other practices, there's a more formal system where they have official counsellors.

It's surprising how seldom people make the connection between the death and the present problems, after a few months have gone by. It's so obvious to the outside observer, and so difficult to comprehend for the person experiencing that problem.

A medical consultation will help to get the problem sorted out. It helps, if you've got problems like bedwetting, behaviour problems, to make sure that the child is medically OK. That takes about five seconds, usually. But the fact is that somebody outside the family has made that decision: 'We haven't got a medical disease, here. Perhaps you're still both of you upset about the death.' An opportunity then arises for you to talk about it.

The person who needs the treatment is not usually the child. It's the mother or father (usually the mother) who needs an opportunity to talk about their feelings; but the child too needs to be considered. And the best way is to help the mother understand that the child has fears, and is expressing them in behaviour, rather than in speech, because the child hasn't got enough speech. Grown-ups don't do that anyway – they express in their behaviour their deepest emotions. Most people come to understand it anyway, I find, in time, and if you can just satisfy them they're not neglecting the other child's medical problems and allow them to talk to one another and to behave like mother and child still, it settles down – after some months. There's always a lasting regret, a memory, an effect of the death on your life, because there always will be.

I asked Miss S., a Health Visitor, how she would help if there seemed to be difficulties between parents and children and she replied that by sitting and chatting, one could usually find a reason for problems between a mother and her child. If both the child and the mother were unhappy a vicious circle was created, and it was far better if she could get their confidence, so that they could discuss with her what the problem was. Once they did, and once the problem was shared, then she could usually act constructively. The mother might be not very well herself, or simply overtired, in which case Miss S. would try to get her some extra help. However, if she could not solve the problem herself, she would ask the mother's permission to refer her to a Child Guidance worker.

The advantage of a consultation with Child Guidance is that they can see the family on a one-to-one basis, sometimes the whole family, and have the time for more case study. Sometimes the Health Visitor, doctor and counsellor work together as a team. In the case of a child over five, it might be their school who recommends that the family be referred to Child Guidance, if they recognize that there are difficulties. However, if the mother is concerned that there are acute difficulties, she can by-pass doctor, Health Visitor and school and contact the Child Guidance clinic, without reference to anyone else.

I asked Mrs S., a Child Guidance Social Worker, about the particular problems that children may have, and she told me that one of the principal problems is that they are likely to be feeling guilty in some way.

When a new baby is born, the existing children may feel badly about it, but they may feel it is taboo to feel that way about a baby, who is supposedly deserving of only warm and affectionate feelings. They therefore feel very guilty, and then, if the baby actually does die, some children, particularly those of certain ages, may think it's their fault, because in some magical way they have caused the death by their bad feelings.

Children are likely to have such assumptions about their own powers, perhaps up to the age of eight, though even adults have such feelings to a certain extent. Obviously, they are more pronounced in a child – an adult is capable of rationalizing, of talking it over and getting it out of their system. Mrs S. said that in order to help a child do the same thing, it is necessary to address the problem directly, that is, to give them permission to have such feelings.

Similarly, where a child is very insecure about its parents, it is a good idea to bring the possible bad feelings that it had, out into the open. If it feels that by its thoughts it could cause the death or disappearance of its baby brother or sister, then its own power is a frightening thing and potentially capable of removing its parents after an argument.

Mrs S. suggested that parents say something like: 'I expect you felt cross with the baby sometimes, or angry that Mummy was cuddling her and didn't have too much time for you. Perhaps you think that something happened to the baby because of your feelings. But this wouldn't happen. We all have bad feelings, all the time, and we don't make people go away.'

Not only do you reassure the child about his or her 'magical' abilities, but this way you are telling the child that it is acceptable to have bad feelings and that you are not horrified by them. Removing their feelings of guilt may take a load off their shoulders.

The child may feel grief as well as guilt.

Babies always come carrying love. (A mother feels this when she has a baby who is a 'good' baby. An insecure mother can feel very secure for the length of time a baby is a baby.) It carries uncritical love; a child would see it that way. So the child has loving feelings towards the baby even in spite of its bad feelings; and it's not just the feelings that the child has for the baby, but the feeling that the baby is a *source* of love for the child. Therefore, if you have a source of love and that source of love goes, the child is likely to feel grief, as well as guilt. It depends a little, of course, on how quickly the cot death happens. Also, if there has been a great deal of build-up.

More than anything else, the older child is bound up with the mother, so that the mother's grief is very much a part of the child's. So the closeness of the relationship to the mother might equally play a part. The child would share in the distress of the mother. The first child particularly has an intense relationship with its parents.

Recalling Tracey's behaviour at the time of her brother's death, I asked Mrs S. if 'acting out' the death was a good way for children to express their feelings.

I think it's an excellent way. They are also telling us they understand what's going on. So often someone will say of a two-year-old, 'Well, they never realized, anyway.' Say, the baby dies in hospital, and nobody's told the child; things can be hidden from children, and yet the child will show by its actions that it does know what's going on.

I asked if the child who showed very little reaction was an exception.

No, but it's waiting for the parents to talk about it. If the parents' reaction is very immense, then the child's got to repress his or her own reaction, because there isn't room for it. So often, the child will bottle things up, because it has to be strong to support the parent, and this does mean that a reaction is not allowed. It is very important for all the family to talk about it. The child may be able to accept it as a matter of fact, but it's certainly important that the subject is discussed, because if it is not discussed, there are all sorts of things which might be going on in that child's mind, mixed up with what's happening.

The child may simply feel insecure, as perhaps the parent does, in that you cannot count on the normality and stability of life any longer. In this case, it is a good idea to bring normality into the child's life and make things structured and regular, and try to restore the child's confidence about life returning to normal, even though you are still telling him or her that you still feel sad about the baby. Once again, it is important to reassure him that everyone else in the family is quite safe, and that you do not expect other disasters to happen. Stress that the baby was simply not strong enough to survive.

Another reaction suggested to me by Dr Emanual Lewis of the Perinatal Bereavement Unit, Tavistock Clinic, London was that a child might feel very inadequate because he could not make his mother happy again. However lively or clever he was, he was never good enough. Speaking specifically of my own case, Dr Lewis said:

It's very hard if your mother is very upset at having miscarriages and a dead baby, because you're meant to be the idol of her eye, or you'd like to feel that. If you're really capable, then your mother would be happy whether she had another baby or not. There's a sense of: 'I wish I could make my mother better; if I was really a nice boy, she wouldn't be so sad.'

Mrs S. suggested that even if a child is not showing a severe reaction, it might be worth while taking him to Child Guidance about three months after the death for a general chat, just to make sure that everything is all right.

Reactions of older children

Mrs S. said that children from five to nine years might appear very callous and parents might be irritated by this. Marian gave an example of this when describing how her children seemed fairly relaxed when she was expecting another baby. 'Whether they weren't, inside, and they didn't ever say anything to me, I don't know. Sometimes they played games concerned with the baby's death.' Once, one of the children said something hurtful and upset Marian, but he obviously did not mean it. However, sometimes they would realize that certain things upset their mother and would be more cautious about what they said.

A particular effect of the death on an older child might be that a girl approaching puberty might lose faith in her own ability to produce a healthy child.

Pam's daughter, Amanda, who was nearly eleven at the time of her brother Nicholas's death, did not talk about it a great deal. However, about eight months later, when Pam was pregnant again, a teacher found Amanda crying at school and made a point of telling Pam about it. Amanda was worried about her mother; she was worried about the new baby to be born soon, and wondered whether everything would be repeated.

Amanda's younger brother Tim, eight-and-a-half years old, did not show a lot of reaction either, but appeared well adjusted to the situation. He would always go to his mother if he heard her crying and, unlike Amanda, in later days was more likely to speak of baby Nicholas as a person.

Some years have passed since their brother's death. Amanda, now a young woman, shows no interest in getting married or having children, and it is difficult to know whether this is a result of her experience of cot death, or perhaps her reaction to the sister born after the death, whereas Tim is getting married and has in the past expressed a desire to have a family.

The surviving twin

Despite the fact that the death of one twin may not have been discussed in the survivor's presence, or perhaps even because of that, the surviving twin may experience problems as it grows older, and Dr Bryan stresses in her article that 'all single surviving twins should hear about their twin from the start and be encouraged to ask questions and express their feelings, rational or not'. She continues:

Many feel angry with the twin for deserting them; for causing such unhappiness in the family; for making them, the survivors, feel guilty. They may also feel anger towards their parents for 'allowing' the twin to die. Some have secret fantasies which can be frightening and indeed dangerous if allowed to develop.

Parents may also have angry and resentful feelings for the survivor.

Parents' feelings towards surviving children

Though many of the parents I spoke to felt they were short of patience with their surviving children, very few seem to have experienced the emotions that I felt towards my four-year-old-son. Only Lynne seemed to feel the same way as I did. She, like me had found it difficult to get on with her older child after the baby's death. 'I almost resented him,' she said. 'Everyone said, "Aren't you lucky you've got another one". But he was not the one I wanted. I didn't want him – I wanted Andrew.'

I had similar feelings, which I knew at the time were quite irrational. I knew very well that if the situation were reversed and the baby had survived and my son had died, I would be feeling equally angry and irritated by the baby. Nevertheless, I could not quell my feelings of irritation towards my son. Even in spite of the successful outcome of my next pregnancy, I am not convinced that I was able to give him the love and warmth that he deserved, for many years. Some of these feelings may not have been related to the cot death. Some may have been directly concerned with my irritation at the boisterous nature of small boys, particularly during those early years when they do not seem to respond to logical reasons for not doing naughty/adventurous/noisy things. Some of my feelings may have been brought about by the fact that he was the survivor when two early miscarriages occurred, as well as when my baby girl died, or it may simply have been that the strain of those several years caused me to vent my anger on the person who was with me more than anyone else.

Whatever the reason, I would urge mothers with aggressive feelings towards their surviving children to seek help, so that many years afterwards, they are not asking themselves how much emotional damage they may have inflicted upon an innocent and lovable person. This is such an important matter to me that I spent a long time discussing it with Mrs S. She said that it is normal to feel anger at a death. Some people feel angry with the person who has left them; however, it seems unacceptable to focus anger on a baby, so one focuses the anger elsewhere. It may be, as seemed to be the case with me, that the other child becomes the recipient of that anger; with other people, it might be the husband or wife who is the focal point. Sometimes if there is no one to be angry with, the anger becomes focused on oneself and causes a deep depression.

Help from Child Guidance

I asked Mrs S. if, recognizing my own inability to get on with my son, I should have sought help.

I think you should have referred yourself to a Child Guidance Clinic. Mothers can go direct to Child Guidance Clinics, and particularly around the time of a death, I think it is very helpful.

If you've got a small child and you've got feelings you don't like, it can be helpful to talk over them and perhaps work through them, whereas *you* were struggling with them all the time and having to take a long time to work it out.

I asked, 'If the mother had reached a stage of anger with her child where she was smacking it unnecessarily, and then decided to refer herself to the Child Guidance Clinic, would her child be in danger of being taken into care?'

She replied:

First of all, children are only taken into care in the last possible situation. Children are not taken into care from Child Guidance; the whole idea about Child Guidance is to help people work through the problems – not to deal with them in a high-handed fashion. And it's always confidential. Obviously, if there was a suspicion that there was a 'non-accidental injury', in other words, the child had a broken arm or very severe bruising (or whatever), then one would say that the Social Services would have to be notified, because that's the law. There may have to be a case conference around it, but we will try and help sort this out. Even in a 'non-accidental injury' situation, hopefully, once parents are getting help, it won't occur again, because they won't feel the whole brunt of it is falling on them.

Mrs S. was in complete agreement with my suggestion that if a parent went for Child Guidance early enough, this situation might be completely avoided. She was also careful to point out that smacking your child unnecessarily is *not* the same as 'non-accidental injury', whereas breaking a child's arm *is*.

We have all smacked our children! But it could *escalate* into 'non-accidental injury' and so it is very, very important that you do get professional help – and the Child Guidance Clinic is geared to that – to help you sort out your feelings and the feelings of the child. Maybe extra time at a nursery would be a help. It would give the mother a bit more space – more time to be on her own.

I suggested to Mrs S. that it was difficult to confess to having unpleasant feelings towards your own child.

I think the most important thing is to feel that Child Guidance understands; we have very good psychiatrists and social psychologists and psychiatric social workers. Often, we have quite an 'elderly' social worker population, which means that most of us have children of our own and are aware, not only from textbooks, but from our own experience, of the kind of feelings people have (and that with understanding and not criticism).

You always have to screw up your courage to go for the first time, but it's very important, because guilt is the most destructive emotion that there is; far more destructive in some ways than anger. And you can be *absolved* from your guilt. You can then work at what the problem is.

Most Child Guidance Clinics are in the telephone book, and, as stated, you can go direct if you like, without reference to your doctor or Health Visitor. But you could also talk to your doctor or Health Visitor and tell them you would like some help from the Child Guidance Clinic. Mrs S. commented:

Some clinics have waiting lists; some don't; some have 'out' visits; some don't. Some clinics do family therapy; no clinic operates in the same way. You will find a tremendous difference between one and another. The only thing one can say is that I don't think any visit to the clinic would be unhelpful; you can reject it; it's voluntary; if you go along and don't like the sort of response you get, then you don't come back again. So, you've lost nothing by trying it. Personalities vary!

A stitch in time saves nine; it's really terribly appropriate to problems with children. I just beg all parents to come early with their problems and not wait.

It's important that you get that intervention and don't just say, 'Well, this is something I've got to struggle with on my own.'

And it is surprising what a short time it needs. Quite often, a few visits to talk things over and get a bit more insight will sort out the problem and help everyone. The sad thing is when people don't come, when they could have done, and then perhaps the relationship has gone on and deteriorated and they end up with teenage rows.

Mrs S. stressed once again:

Please come in at the beginning of the problem, because the sadness of leaving the problem unsolved is so great.

Guilt

To take action to solve the above problems is obviously constructive, but to torture oneself with guilt is not.

For whatever reason, just like the children, the majority of people feel guilty at the death of someone to whom they have been close. Invariably they find themselves wishing that they had been kinder to that person, had visited them more often, etc. Perhaps in their hearts they feel guilty that they are alive, and glad of it, and the other person is dead. Perhaps, it is simply that they feel they can now never put to rights any wrong they did to that person. Whatever the reason, it seems to be a very normal reaction. In the case of the death of a baby, the mother seems to feel that guilt even more acutely, since it is closely tied up with her instinctive feeling that initially the baby's care was almost totally in her hands.

Strange though it may seem, I had similar feelings of guilt about the two early miscarriages I experienced. I felt as if I had not done enough to protect those babies, even at that early stage. Perhaps for this reason, I was prepared for my guilt feelings and, since I was aware of their destructive nature, I tried to put them from my mind, though not always successfully, for they would frequently arise to torture me.

Whereas, in the early days, the guilt was perhaps very irrational, as time passed and my knowledge of the subject of cot death grew, so my guilt was more likely to be triggered off by a well-informed report. When, for example, some years after Amanda's death, I read one of the first reports that over-heating might be one of the possible factors in some cot deaths, I was overwhelmed with guilt. I realized that in my concern for Amanda because she had had a cold, I had almost certainly covered her with too many blankets in a warm house.

Maureen A. said that she felt guilty about absolutely everything, rational and irrational things alike.

I did feel that if I had been out driving, for example, and I'd made a slight error of judgement and there'd been an accident and somebody had been hurt, I would have been held to be responsible for that. (The police would have had me for dangerous driving, or careless driving, or manslaughter, if someone had been killed.) And I really couldn't see that logically it wasn't the same sort of position – that a baby is so helpless and tiny and so dependent upon other people that somehow it had to be my fault that this awful thing had happened. I went back over everything and thought, 'Well, if only I'd done it differently'. I think in that way, it was a help having another baby, because some of the things I *did* do the same – deliberately the same, almost – chancing my arm, and she (Julie) was all right.

The thing that stuck in my mind and affected me afterwards, was that we had been to a particular supermarket the day before. I would not take Julie into that supermarket when she was a baby. I kept feeling, 'If I hadn't taken him to this nasty shop full of germs and people breathing all over him, it would have been all right.'

Sue too kept asking herself what she had done that was different; and in addition to her early worries, she also felt guilty because, on the occasion of Anthony's death, Neville had not yet returned from the allotment to witness her putting the baby to bed, so in her mind he could not know definitely that everything had been all right at that time. However, Neville certainly did not feel she had any reason to think that way. 'To the best of my knowledge, we had done nothing different with Anthony than we had with Tracey,' he said. He felt the guilt was all in Sue's mind.

Lynne had not had great feelings of guilt, though initially she worried that Andrew might have got too cold after a bath. Subsequently, she did feel guilty that she had not gone into him when he had cried in the night.

Maureen B. felt particularly guilty, even after several years, when she read a new report in the papers mentioning links between cot deaths and smoking mothers, because she had not given up smoking during pregnancy. Her feelings of guilt about that and about not breast feeding created a barrier between her and her husband and she found it difficult to talk about it to him.

Tony never approved of anybody smoking during pregnancy anyway; so I felt doubly guilty that way, almost as though I'd killed his child. Also, it was my decision not to breast feed; it's not as if I tried to breast feed and couldn't for some reason; I just said I didn't want to.

Sadly, the very fact that Maureen did not have another daughter probably reinforced her feelings of guilt.

I really felt as if there was a God there and He had given me a daughter and taken her away as some sort of punishment.

What Mrs S. says about guilt applies to all situations – guilt is a destructive emotion. It contributes nothing and torments the recipient.

If one returns to Maureen's comparison with careless driving, one has to remember that a driver is required by law to take a test before he is allowed on the road. In the Highway Code he can learn by heart what he is and is not allowed to do. If he is careless on the road, the likelihood is that he has disobeyed one of the rules. But parents do not have rules to follow. They may read books or articles, sometimes with conflicting advice. They may listen to friends or neighbours whose advice may or may not be informed. A generation of conscientious parents failed to immunize their children against whooping cough for the best of reasons. Pregnant women were for a short period warned against eating potatoes, and even against staying in the kitchen when they were boiling! Parents have to use their own judgement about such warnings, and when they see other babies thriving despite the fact that their mothers have not followed all recommendations, they may not believe that their own babies will be harmed if they ignore those recommendations themselves, and in some cases, they may be right.

In addition, there are so many areas of parenthood in which we undoubtedly do make mistakes, some of which have no effect upon our children's lives at all, and some of which can easily be remedied, that we have to learn to forgive ourselves for the actions we have or have not taken, which do ultimately seem to have made some contribution to an eventual tragic outcome. We do not intend our children to be harmed, and whatever errors we make, we do not believe that they will have the effect that they do. If we can eventually make some good come out of the terrible event, it is sometimes easier to forgive ourselves and put aside the guilt.

7 Looking inward – looking outward

After the first few months have passed, parents may need less outward expression of their feelings, and may have less need to talk to others. However, they will probably give a great deal of thought to the tragedy. I found that there were times when thinking about Amanda's death was too painful and I had to try and blot it out by listening to the radio and taking my mind off it in various ways. But there were also times when I thought a great deal about what had happened to me. Like many other mothers, I looked back at what seemed like a year of my life totally wasted and I began to feel that I had to create happenings which would ensure that Amanda's birth and death were not wasted and had some meaning.

Only about two or three months after her death, I saw a report of a cot death in the newspaper and Michael contacted the family mentioned and told them of our own case. Later, I sent them literature that I had by now received. When I received a letter thanking me, I felt quite elated, and overwhelmed by the discovery I had made that Amanda's death had not been quite wasted. I felt that the more I could do to help others who were going through the same sadness, the less bitter I would feel.

One day, when walking through my village, I noticed a seat by the bus stop with a plaque on it, which I had never noticed before. When I read it, I found it was an inscription in memory of a young officer who had been killed in the Second World War. I thought of the parents of that young man, who had nothing left but his memory, and how they had wanted to keep his name alive so that people would see it thirty or forty years later, as I had done. In addition, they too had wanted to do something practical, so that people would actually benefit in some way, not just see an empty memorial.

I suppose I realized then that that was what I wanted to do too. I wanted to create a memorial to Amanda, and though it might not be a visible monument, each time I was able to help someone, in my heart I would be saying, 'This is for you, Amanda'. In the course of time, when I began to write letters to other parents and articles for publication, I always tried to include her name. That too was part of the memorial. I remembered seeing a play by Harold Pinter, in which the characters were all in an afterlife. All the while they were remembered on earth, they retained some kind of link with it. Once they were forgotten, they were in effect, cut off. This memory stayed in my mind and it became important to me that Amanda should not be forgotten, irrespective of my future child or children – that she would have a permanent place in my memory, and that her name would be remembered and seen by others too.

As the length of time since the death became greater, my confidence grew that this was the right thing to do. I had always enjoyed writing, but my attempts to get articles and letters on the subject of cot death published, reawakened a desire within me to write professionally. Even after the birth of my second daughter, Karen, I continued to write about my experience, but then with gratitude at my new happiness.

There is always a great deal of concern by doctors that the new baby should not be a 'replacement' for the dead baby. I felt that the writing I did, and the help I gave to other parents all served to establish in my mind a separate identity for Amanda. My living children were cared for in one way. My dead child had a separate part of my life which was devoted exclusively to her. At times, I have no doubt I was quite obsessional in thinking of the good that I had to go and do in the world on her behalf.

Religious feelings

I also thought a great deal about God's role in my experience. At first, I used to ask, 'Why have You done this to me?' Then, as time passed, I began to feel that God was giving me the strength to cope with the sadness. Later, I felt that I had been 'chosen' to carry out what appeared to be particular tasks.

Sometimes it seemed to me that God had caused my daughter to die in order to make me behave as I had done and make some good come out of it, including my desire to write.

At other times, this seemed to be a very terrible view of God, who would put events into people's lives, just to see how they would cope with them. I suppose during the whole period of both pregnancies and both births, I gave a great deal of thought to God and at that time, He seemed very close to me. Only after some time did those feelings begin to abate.

I spoke to other mothers about how they felt the death had affected their lives and, how much religion had entered into it. Pam, who regarded herself as a 'church-going agnostic', said that her feelings of uncertainty changed, following the cot death, to a certainty that there was nothing. She was enraged at the death of her baby, and felt that if there was a God, He was a murderer. However, of recent years she had reverted to her original feelings, possibly being less agnostic than before, perhaps because she has now been able to see some purpose to the tragedy.

Marian's family seemed to gain a great deal of comfort from their religion. When Marian was expecting Nicholas, people used to say to her daughter, 'I expect you're hoping for a sister, aren't you?' and she would reply, 'Oh, I've got a sister, but she's in Heaven.' Later, when, through a Foundation support group, Marian and her children met another mother, who had also lost a daughter named Victoria, she found that her older children were enormously comforted (even after two-and-a-half years) by the idea that the two babies were in Heaven together and that the babies of all the other mothers she had met were all companions for each other.

Pam was comforted at the idea of an elderly friend being 'there' already and looking after the baby.

Jane said she would describe herself and David as 'lapsed Christians', going to church at Christmas, and perhaps a couple of times a year. However, they found that they gravitated to church every Sunday for the first couple of months after Naomi's death, though when they felt better they stopped going so much. Jane found it strange that she should wish to go to church and would have imagined that the death would have weakened her faith, whereas in fact she found it strengthened it.

I asked Maureen if she felt that not being a religious person affected her.

Oh certainly. Because it meant that I had no certainty of an after-life or that the baby had gone on to better things, any of those things which I suppose must be very comforting.

In addition, the attitude of some religious acquaintances was upsetting to her, because they were inclined to say to her, 'Oh, it's for the best,' and she felt it was very wrong of them to assume this.

Outside activities

Many people throw themselves into an activity such as fund-raising or befriending, or writing, as I did, some with similar and some with slightly different motives. Eventually, however, people may continue to participate in the activity for its own sake. Invariably they choose an activity they feel comfortable doing in the first place, and they may come to enjoy this activity. Without having lost sight of their original reason for wanting to do this, it is natural that the intensity of feelings fade, and also natural that people who get involved in a particular project will become interested in it.

By the same token, people may find that there are some things they are totally incapable of tackling, because it simply goes against the grain. I myself found that I was unable to hold a social fund-raising function until two or three years after Amanda's death. I felt that an essential part of a social function to which you invite other people, is to be smiling and relaxed, and I could not be that initially. If the point of the exercise was to raise money for the cause, I could not expect outsiders to come and be subjected to a display of sadness or indoctrination. Only when I did feel detached did I begin to hold an annual 'coffee morning' in my village to raise funds.

However, I have never been a natural 'fund-raiser'. It is no good pretending I could involve myself totally in a great deal of well-organized fund-raising through major events, because I would feel quite uncomfortable doing this. Fortunately, some people feel totally at home in this field, and it is thanks to their efforts that sums of money have been raised for the Foundation for the Study of Infant Deaths.

Many people who have been affected by a tragedy want to do something to help others and find satisfaction in being able to do that. Fortunately, different people are prepared to tackle different aspects of help, which all complement each other. Communicating information, fund-raising, 'befriending' and becoming involved with a support group are all ways of actively helping other people.

Communicating information

Writing, for me, started off with a desire to draw attention to the then little-publicized problem of cot death and in addition, to the organizations available to help parents, so that they would not have to endure the feelings of isolation that I had suffered initially.

People were put in contact with me by relations, by the British Guild for Sudden Infant Death Study and, in addition, I was contacted by a few people as a result of a letter I had written to a newspaper. In the early seventies, I also wrote occasionally to health authorities telling them of the existence of the British Guild and the Foundation, which were not at that time known to them.

When writing to other mothers, I examined my feelings in detail in order to tell them how I felt. The writing of the letters was draining and at the same exhilarating, as all my emotions poured from me. Ostensibly, I did it to help them, but the act of writing was very helpful to me too.

Mandy also derived some comfort from writing and sent me a copy of an article she had had published, saying:

This shows exactly how I felt two-and-a-half years after Sophie's death. I, as a person, at that time needed to put my thoughts on paper, which helped me a great deal and at the same time earned a small amount of money for the Foundation.

Perhaps the sort of articles that Mandy and I and others wrote are less important today, when there is so much more knowledge about cot death, and of the Foundation. But every now and then, the wrong sort of publicity appears in the press, causing anger and distress to many bereaved parents, and it becomes very important then to counter the banner headlines with informed information. In any case, there are always likely to be parents who wish to express their feelings on paper, and others who gain benefit by reading of their experiences.

Fund-raising

In various areas, groups of Friends of the Foundation exist which are well organized and do a great deal of work, both with fund-raising and 'befriending'. Individual parents may prefer to join such groups, where the ability to organize a large function is obviously much greater. However, some parents prefer to do things on their own, as and when they feel able, and the small amounts that regularly trickle in to the Foundation are also valued and needed.

Sue and Neville got extremely involved with fund-raising,

though not until about two years after Anthony died, when they moved to a new area. At this point, they decided to find out more about the Foundation's work, and since they were now in an area where there was a Friends of the Foundation group in existence, they joined the group and worked very hard for it for a few years.

Until that time that group's fund-raising efforts had consisted mainly of jumble sales and coffee mornings, which raised relatively small amounts of money. Then the wives persuaded some of the husbands to get involved and the husbands then helped organize major functions and more adventurous events, raising larger sums of money. During the time that Sue and Neville were there and involved, the group raised ten thousand pounds. Through the group, Sue and Neville also got involved in the 'befriending' of newly bereaved families, and 'getting cot death talked about and talking about it'. After they moved again, their circumstances changed and they ceased to be able to do major fund-raising work, but still sold raffle tickets and Christmas cards and remained available for 'befriending'.

There was a certain satisfaction in having a 'good day' and raising a reasonable amount of money. However, Sue and Neville still felt frustration, that even after all their work, there was still no answer to the question 'Why?' Why had their baby died? I asked them which was more important to them, finding out the cause of cot deaths, or the ability to help others. They both felt quite definitely that finding out the cause was most important and that if, as a result, there was some means of prevention of cot death, then the requirement to help other bereaved parents would no longer be necessary. Helping other people in the meantime was peripheral.

Maureen A. felt she had not done enough in the way of fund-raising.

Rob has run in marathons and that's about the extent of it, apart from helping out at coffee mornings and trying rather half-heartedly to sell a few Christmas cards, but I'm not a very good person at 'pushing' and I found that fairly difficult. But I do feel that really we ought to be doing more.

Maureen had also sold raffle tickets for a separate charity, which raises funds specifically to purchase apnoea monitors and give them out to suitable parents in their area.

I asked Maureen why she thought that fund-raising was important and she replied:

Since there's a fairly prevalent attitude that babies don't matter as much as other people, then it's very unlikely that huge amounts of money are going to be forthcoming from the Government to fund research into it, and it's simply a desire that there should be research to spare other people what we've gone through.

Mandy, too, had held coffee mornings and raised small amounts of money, but Lynne did not feel very comfortable raising funds, nor sending out Foundation Christmas cards, though she was very happy to give help to other mothers.

However, Maureen B. regularly bought the Foundation Christmas cards, though she had not had much contact with the Foundation.

Jane was involved in the sale of Christmas cards and coffee mornings and her feelings were rather similar to mine.

Every time I sell a packet of Christmas cards, or with 'befriending', every time I go and talk to someone, those nine weeks weren't for nothing; *something* has come out of it; her life *had* a purpose. Not doing it would be like trying to close the door and say she didn't exist.

Although, as I have said, my fund-raising efforts have been relatively minor, compared with others, I have not found it too difficult to hold one fund-raising function each year. I held my first 'coffee morning' in my own home and I sold 'good-as-new' items as well as home-made cakes provided by some of my friends; I dropped hand-written notes to all my neighbours, telling them of the sale. On a subsequent occasion, a friend who was nearer the centre of our village offered her own house as a venue. After that, I hired a room in our village hall and advertised the function through the church newsletter and in the local shops. Friends brought me raffle prizes, as well as home produce, and this brought in a little more money.

At first, it needs confidence to ask friends to help and to ask people to come along. My confidence has grown a little, in that respect, and similarly I am less shy about asking people if they would like to buy Christmas cards. For the last ten years, I have regularly had the help of about half a dozen friends who have not experienced a cot death, as well as the cot death mothers who have joined me in the last few years.

The effect of this regular event is that I am now known as a contact, and I have been asked on a few occasions for literature, or the Foundation address, for people in other districts.

Though running a coffee morning is a traditional and fairly easy event to organize, people have had other good ideas, which have raised from small sums to extremely large amounts.

One 'Friend of the Foundation' is collecting used postage stamps, various sponsored functions have been held, from sponsored swims and walks to sponsored hot air balloon events. The sale of Christmas cards grew from a small to a large fund-raiser. One mother whose professional work is in public relations became Chairwoman of the Foundation's Appeals Committee, and organized the children's 'Design a Christmas Card Competition' in collaboration with W. H. Smith and the Trustee Savings Bank. Now solely sponsored by W. H. Smith, it raises more than £100,000 each year. Parents have been able to raise funds by interesting a 'show-business name' in the cause or by obtaining sponsorship from large companies. Not only parents but grandparents have been instigators of events, and one grandmother has been the co-producer of two highly successful recipe books which have raised large amounts of money for the Foundation.

'Befrienders' and support groups

The Foundation tries carefully to select 'befrienders' who have reached the stage where they can be of real help to the newly bereaved. Part of their leaflet giving guidelines to prospective 'befrienders' is reproduced below:

Anyone wishing to become a befriender by offering non-professional support to newly bereaved families following a cot death should fulfil the following requirements:
— have suffered the death of their own baby unexpectedly as a cot death
— be a stable caring person motivated primarily by the wish to help others similarly bereaved
— have come to terms with their own grief and be capable of calmly sharing their own experience with the newly bereaved. As a rough guide this usually means that the befriender is at least over the first anniversary of the death of their own child
— be a good listener, allow the bereaved parent to talk about their own experiences
— be capable of suppressing, when necessary, any strong personal beliefs of a controversial, religious or moral nature which might offend or conflict with the view of the family which is being befriended
— be prepared to continue support for as long as the newly bereaved family wants and needs it
— ideally, to have the active support of spouse and family and to be able to offer support as a couple
— be prepared to attend meetings of the local group (where one exists)

- be prepared where necessary to refer difficult cases, especially those needing more help than befriending, to the relevant professional
- never to get involved in medico-legal matters or intervene on behalf of a parent. Parents should be referred back to their own doctors or to their Community Health Council
- never disseminate technical or medical information without checking with the FOUNDATION which keeps up-to-date information

Although in some ways, I felt I was better able to support by writing letters, I also met some mothers who were referred to me by the Health Visitor or some other contact. Initially, I sent or gave these mothers the Foundation literature and address, if they had not already received it, but some felt it helpful to be in contact with me in addition. By this time, two or three years had passed since Amanda's death. I had, of course, given birth to Karen, and I was able to be fairly detached. I had no knowledge of counselling, so I had to use my instincts, and whether these were right or wrong, I cannot say.

I assumed that mothers would want to talk about their experience, so I let them talk, but at the same time, I would sometimes confirm that I had felt the same way, or mention a similar feeling that I had had. I thought that it might be difficult for a bereaved mother to keep asking for help from a semi-stranger, so I often took the initiative. Sometimes I telephoned and asked how the mother was, or if she would like to come over to see me. Sometimes I called in. I took the risk of being a nuisance and hoped that I would recognize it, when I was no longer needed.

Mandy wrote:

I support any bereaved parents I hear about in this area, making friends and just listening to their fears and showing them that I have come through the other side of this nightmare. I phone and leave my number and if they wish to speak to someone that has suffered a similar tragedy and who really knows how it feels, they can ring me any time. During the last nine years I have visited quite a few bereaved mums and they have all been pleased for me to listen to their experience.

Sue was not sure how much satisfaction she had gained from 'befriending' others, though she had probably benefited herself from talking through the tragedy and finding out that she shared the emotions of anger, hurt and frustration with others. However, she did feel satisfaction and pleasure when another mother wrote to thank her for help, and subsequently to tell her of the birth of another baby. She felt 'on top of the world' when she heard of the birth. After eight years, Sue found it increasingly difficult to reassure newly bereaved parents. It was tempting to say, 'You'll get over it'. She did not feel she could give the same help as she had originally.

Jane also found it difficult to reassure other mothers when she was herself seven months pregnant.

Lynne had left the area where her cot death occurred, before starting to act as a 'befriender' herself, but she was ready to do this in her new area.

Pam was still very much involved in the organization of a local support group. Though she had always felt there was a need for it, she had not actually started up this group herself but had taken it over after the mother who had started it became ill. Pam felt that her own recovery would have taken place much earlier if she had been the instigator of the group. However, that was not her personality – she tended to be someone who did what was asked of her, rather than a prime mover. However, when nine years had passed since the death, she completely forgot the anniversary, because she was so involved with other cot death parents.

Surprisingly, Pam said that her mother still thought that she dwelt upon the cot death too much, by doing the work she did in running the support group. Her mother thought it was 'keeping her upset'. However, Pam said that she enjoyed doing the work and it had helped heal the wounds.

Even when people have had other babies, Pam found that there was still a need to talk about the various emotions, and a support group such as hers provided opportunities for mothers to meet and find someone prepared to listen.

Marian, though her own experience of cot death was more recent, has also become involved in supporting other parents. She said:

You're very concerned to try to pass on to other people the lessons that you've learned, which aren't necessarily through cot death, but from any tragic experience.

In the end, I think that almost everyone who has had something to give of themselves, through their time and effort, whether through fund-raising, 'befriending' or any other means are more likely to feel that their baby's death was not entirely in vain and less likely to be permanently embittered by their experience.

8 The next pregnancy

Another baby?

The decision as to whether or not to have another baby is one that is likely to be uppermost from the earliest days after the death, followed closely by the question, 'How soon?' I remember asking the visiting doctor that question on the day after Amanda's death. When she suggested that physically, there was no reason why I should wait, but that I 'might make a "replacement" out of a new baby', I felt that that 'permission' was good enough for me. I felt strongly that I could handle the emotional problems, and that nine months was long enough to wait for another baby (if I were fortunate enough to conceive immediately) and long enough to mourn.

Sue however, was not confident in her ability to cope emotionally with a further pregnancy. She said:

Physically, I could have conceived another baby within six months; mentally, I don't think I could have coped.

We were told by lots of people locally, 'You'll feel better as soon as you're pregnant again'. 'You're young; have another one immediately.'

Sue said that although she would have liked a larger family, she was not sure if it would have helped at the time, and when a long time afterwards, she did want another baby, Neville did not. Neville confirmed that he was reluctant to have any more children. 'I didn't think that I could cope. I couldn't have coped if anything had gone wrong with another baby.'

My husband Michael had reservations about my desire to become pregnant again very soon after the last pregnancy, but I was overwhelmed by the very powerful desire to have another baby as soon as possible. This desire was further fuelled by the fact that I had already suffered two early miscarriages, and further delays afterwards, in order to recover physically and safeguard the next pregnancy. My son was now nearly four years old and my hopes of providing him with a companion near his age were receding all the time.

Another mother, who was more desperate than I was and whom I met at a support group, was in her late thirties with a twleve-year gap between her only child and the dead baby. Sadly, she had had a Caesarian delivery and had been sterilized at the same time. When her baby died, she had no doubt whatsoever that she would have to have a reversal of the sterilization, even if she failed to have another baby.

It was necessary to delay the reversal operation, to give her body time to recover from the Caesarian. Finally, it had taken place three months after the death of her baby, and had been successful. However, so far, no pregnancy had occurred. She was aware that, at her age, she might be less fertile than a younger woman, and her desperation to have another baby was increased by the feeling that she might not have too many potential child-bearing years left. She felt she was racing against time. The desire to have another baby obsessed her, so that she felt she could not get on with any other aspect of her life, until she had achieved her objective. Since the death of her baby, she had taken up gardening as a hobby and this perhaps satisfied some creative need in her.

Another mother whom I met at the same time, and who for various reasons had decided against another pregnancy, had also experienced this yearning for another baby, but found that it had abated in time.

Alice, a mother of two, who did not have another baby after the death of her daughter, became a mature student, eventually achieving a Master's degree after several years of study. She found that many of the people with whom she started out at college were there as a result of some sort of 'life crisis', including bereavement.

Those people who cannot or decide not to have another baby may feel the need of a new interest or career or some form of creativity, which can take almost any form, from oil painting to house-painting.

Lynne would have liked another baby as soon as possible though in fact, it was a year before her next baby was conceived, because of physical problems. She found this a long wait. She felt she was being regarded as a 'neurotic female, who, if she calmed down and stopped flapping, would be all right'. However, only after treatment of the physical problems did she conceive.

Maureen A. did not want to wait for another baby. She said that her first pregnancy and birth had been very difficult and had put her off having further children, and that she was merely responding to social and other pressures in having a second pregnancy. Nevertheless, the day that Timothy died she said that she wanted another baby. Though she did not want to wait, it was some time before she conceived, and she got impatient and upset as a result of this delay. Eventually, about nine months after the baby's death, she rather reluctantly went to the doctor and was put on a very low dose of Valium.

I really didn't want to because I thought that it wasn't going to help. By the time I ended up taking the Valium, I was in an awful state at not being pregnant again and felt that time was slipping by and Nicholas was getting older. It did calm me down to the extent that it didn't worry me so much, and then I did become pregnant.

Maureen B. wanted another baby almost immediately, in spite of the fact that Tony had had a vasectomy. Tony himself was unwilling to have the vasectomy reversed though he would have been happy if Maureen had become pregnant during the period before the vasectomy took effect. When she asked the doctor if there was any chance of Tony having a reversal, he told her he did not think there was any chance whatsoever. However, she did not have a great deal of confidence in her doctor and continued to try and find out about this possibility, despite Tony's reluctance. It was well over a year before her husband had the reversal, and during that time life returned to some form of normality. 'The worst times were seeing other little girls, or other little babies really, but mainly girls. And I suppose there was always that hope that I'd persuade him.'

Jane said that she was told by endless people not to rush in and have another baby, but she did nevertheless. She was sure that her decision was the right one. She felt that if she had left it a couple of years, as everyone suggested, she would not have become pregnant at all.

I would have shut that door, and I would have got on with my life and then I would have said, 'I'm not going to allow myself to be open to this sort of hurt again. I'm not going to have another one.'
Everybody said to me – everybody, without fail – 'Leave it – do *not* have another one. Give yourself time to recover.' But I still say that it was the best thing I could have done, because if I had left it, I know that I personally would never have done it.

Jane did not accept the advice, and she sought me out, soon after Naomi's death, purely because I was a mother who had had another baby. Prior to meeting me, she had made contact with another 'befriender' who had not. In some ways, this story confirms my feelings that mothers tend to follow their own instincts and I asked Dr G. what he felt about this.

I'm a strong believer in following instincts; I think they are probably there for a good reason. But I think a mother should know quite clearly what she's doing and why. She should have her own reasons clear in her mind. She mustn't expect a new baby to replace the old one. It doesn't work like that. She's not just going to have a baby; she's going to have a human being, who's going to grow up into an adult. Is she prepared for that change to take place? Is she going to let this new child develop in a different way? It may well be a different sex – a different kind of baby with a different name – and it's got to be permitted to grow beyond the stage that the previous baby got to.

I'm not terribly impressed by most of the psychological analyses of people's behaviour in this respect. I find them spurious; I think they're just the psychologists' theories and there's very little hard evidence to show how people should or should not behave. I think if you want advice on how people should behave, look around at how people *do* behave. I can tell you how you should behave in order to look after your health, but in order to balance your emotions and lead a contented life, look around at those people who lead contented lives and see what they do – they do it all sorts of different ways.

In practice, I find that couples make their own usually pretty sensible decisions about this. They nearly always do wait a little bit to allow for the initial shock. I would have thought if the pregnancy started within the year, I can't see the harm in that. It doesn't seem too early. As long as she's well physically, and there's no reason to suppose otherwise.

You've just had a pregnancy – allow yourself a few months for your body to recover – even a year, but you may not want to wait as long as that – that's understandable. But give your body a chance to recover from being pregnant. Because it was nine months of fairly strenuous activity, as far as your body was concerned. Then, you yourselves, as a couple, make a decision as to when you want to increase your family.

Dr C. did not see any reason for a long wait, although he pointed out that there should always be some delay after an 'obstetric emergency'. In fact, the older the baby, the less reason there would be to delay, from a physical point of view.
However, of the mothers whom I met, a mother who had lost a six-month-old baby, was one of the only ones who did not want another baby straight away, but preferred to wait. She felt she needed time to mourn her lost daughter.

I, like Jane, did have my next baby very quickly, just over one year after Amanda's birth. I did feel extremely tired for a long time afterwards, and I think that mothers should be advised by their doctors as to whether they are physically ready to go through pregnancy and birth again.

Dr Emanual Lewis of the Perinatal Bereavement Unit felt it could have been an unwise decision on my part to become pregnant so quickly. In papers he has written on the subject of inhibition of mourning during pregnancy, he points out that the effect of having a pregnancy too quickly after any death, is that mourning may be curtailed before it is really completed. This is because given the choice of concentrating her thoughts on the dead baby (or person) or the baby that is to be born, the mother may well opt for thoughts of the future baby, leaving the other child unmourned. The failure to mourn properly may put the mother at psychological risk, which may subsequently affect the relationship with her children. In my own case, I felt I had concentrated on mourning Amanda, and in fact had been afraid to look forward to the new baby, but this may have been partly because of the unusual circumstances of my previous failed pregnancies.

In his paper, Dr Lewis quotes cases where a mother who does not mourn her lost child properly, has rejected or harmed either the new baby after its arrival, or other surviving children of the family.

'Replacement' baby

Dr Lewis was also concerned about cases where a mother becomes pregnant about three months after the birth of the cot death baby, causing her to have her subsequent child on or near the anniversary of the earlier birth. In these cases, the problem is likely to be caused by the inability to differentiate between the two babies, or the belief that the latter is a reincarnation of the former. This too could result in inadequate mourning. Once again, I personally felt that my two babies were separated in my mind, perhaps particularly by my way of writing down my experiences.

Nevertheless, Dr Lewis felt that from a psychological point of view it was unwise to have a baby too quickly, particularly if it caused the new baby to be born on the anniversary of the dead baby's birth or death. He thought that many doctors tended to encourage mothers to have another baby too quickly and felt that they should be telling them to wait. He agreed that in some circumstances, for example when a mother was in her late thirties or early forties and perhaps had no previous children, it was very hard to expect her to hold back. But most people were

in their twenties or early thirties and could afford to wait a year
or two.

'What we particularly want to avoid is what you did, actually,'
Dr Lewis told me, referring to the birth one year later of my
second daughter, in the same month as her sister was born.

It increases the difficulty of separating out the dead baby from the live
baby . . . But it's always hard to be a replacement child, for the parents
and for the child, *always*. So whether they (the parents) waste no time
at all, or whether they wait a couple of years, say, which might be a
good sort of guess at a time, there is still going to be the problem of
the replacement child. It's always going to be a replacement child. But
it may not have parents who are still going through the grieving
process for the first child. It's a replacement, without being a
replacement for the grieving.

Now, I'm not saying that *you* haven't succeeded but, as I have
written, it's very hard for most people to grieve, who have lost a baby
or anyone during pregnancy, particularly in the second and third
trimesters. There is a problem. And *you* say you've solved it, which
some may do, by grieving, but then you have this conflict, I think,
which you may have overcome, of not preparing yourself for the live
baby.

Stillbirth or neonatal death are more extreme cases of any child
death, but the problems of how long to wait and how long to grieve
and the problem of the replacement child are there, whenever the
death occurs, or even when a child replaces the death of an adult.

In Dr Lewis's papers, he suggests that the replacement baby
may be treated as a poor substitute for the idealized dead baby.
However, he also pointed out that the new baby itself may be
idealized.

It's bad to be seen as a marvellous special person, who's a
reincarnation of an idealized person. That's one problem of the
replacement child. The siblings of the replacement – they've got to
cope with this marvellous child. Equally, that's what happens when a
baby dies and he's not well grieved; dead babies tend to be angel
babies, who are idealized. The replacement could either be a
marvellous idealized replacement or it could be denigrated as nowhere
as good. Dead children are no trouble. So when the child angers you,
you feel: 'The adored dead sibling was wonderful, and marvellous and
no trouble to me, whereas you're this pain in the neck.' That feeling is
always there a bit, but it can get quite persistent or cogent, sometimes.

So the replacement child has all sorts of either idealized or
denigrated views of itself, depending on what the mother feels about
the dead baby.

Siblings get caught up either way; either the live sibling is as bad as
the dead one, or as bad as the other surviving one. All these little

subtle things, if they're there in a small degree, make up the differences in a family, and these differences make life more interesting. But if they're extreme, they muddle and distort people. So it affects our personality inevitably, whatever one does, whatever the sequence is, but it's a matter of how much it changes our personality – how much it really places an enormous burden on our personality.

I asked how ideally one would grieve for a baby properly.

It takes time, one or two years is the minimum time that most people take to do a good job on grieving. It's obviously never over; you never stop grieving for someone that's died, but the really hard work is done in the first year or two for most people.

I spoke of the sadness that I felt some years after Michael and I decided that we would not have any more children. He replied:

The risk that you take, if you have neglected some of the grieving, is that with subsequent losses (you have just spoken to me of one loss – not having another child is a sort of loss, being menopausal is a sort of loss) or then if anybody else dies, you may find it harder than you might have done. That's one of the risks of not really grieving for a dead person, that years later, when there's a loss, then it's harder, for you have to grieve for the dead person and start grieving again for the baby (or other person). It's unfinished business – not that there isn't some unfinished business in you, there is. There's unfinished business in everyone, which goes back to losing one's baby relationship with one's mother.

Though doctors may, like Dr Lewis, be concerned that mothers are trying to 'replace' the dead baby, very often the desire for the baby is also prompted by whatever was the motivation for having the last baby. If, for example, the family was considered incomplete, as in my own case, that situation still remains. In the case of the loss of a first baby, then certainly if the young couple originally wanted children, then they are likely to go on wanting them. However, some parents who have an unplanned pregnancy and then lose the baby they regard as a 'bonus baby', still feel the need for another baby afterwards.

Marian and John had not planned to have baby Victoria; however, once they had lost her, they did feel that they definitely wanted another baby. And once baby Nicholas was born, Marian felt that he was extra special and that there was a purpose for him to be born. Despite occasional panics, she felt he was in a way 'protected' and he would not be snatched away from her.

Pam, who originally thought that people should have only

two children because of the world situation, felt that her son was a bonus that she hadn't felt she should allow herself, but was only too pleased to have. 'He was snatched away, so I jumped in with both feet and had another baby.' This was in spite of feelings that she was tempting fate. However, once the pregnancy was under way, she did have moments of doubt as to whether it was the right thing to do.

Some parents are worried about beng 'disloyal' to the dead baby and initially I was concerned about that myself. At the time of Amanda's death, I wanted reassurance that I was 'allowed' to want another baby so badly and I was very relieved when I wrote to another cot death mother, to find that she was expecting another baby. It seems to me now that if the memory of the lost baby is preserved and not pushed aside as if it were something shameful, then to have further children is not being disloyal.

Just as some mothers are worried about admitting that they would like another baby, there are other mothers who feel pressured by all around them, to have another baby which they do not necessarily want. Family and friends are all eager to see the end of the couple's unhappiness and regard another baby as the panacea to cure all ills and bring about the happy ending to the story. Alice was resentful of the fact that baby deaths were 'minimized', and in a letter to the press wrote of her feelings that 'women are advised to "have another one", as if a doll has been broken and needs replacing'. She and her husband did not regret their decision and felt it was absolutely right for them.

However much one may dislike the word 'replacement', there is no doubt that some parents do want a replacement of the baby they have lost. When a baby is born, it is a small cuddly creature that parents want to love and make a fuss of. When a tragedy happens and it dies, the parents are not trying to replace a strongly developed personality, temperament, artistic nature, sense of humour, quick wit, or any of those traits which develop at a later stage. Usually they want merely to have again a very small child that they can love and that is part of them, and for many people the sex of the child or perhaps its appearance are the only attributes they hope might be the same. Obviously, as a baby gets a little older, and starts responding to its parents, it does have a more definite personality of its own, which cannot be replaced.

Those parents who fail to reproduce the baby they hoped for will perhaps always harbour a sadness which is not totally mitigated by the birth of the next baby. If their hopes are set on a baby of a particular sex, they may even eventually regret their decision to have another child. Those people like myself, who have a baby of the hoped-for sex, and feel that they have finally achieved the family they want, may not always be able to identify completely with the feelings of those who have not.

Parents who have lost one of twins may have the most difficult task in adjusting. In their eyes, their twin babies may have been regarded as an integral part of each other. Once their twins are separated by death, they can never be put together again, and a 'replacement' baby cannot replace that entity. The parents may have regarded their twins as special, and that specialness could never be replaced. Even if they were to have another set of twins, their survivor might always be regarded as incomplete without his or her twin.

Vasectomy or sterilization

It is very, very sad when a cot death occurs after such operations have taken place. For even when the operation was carried out because an unplanned pregnancy occurred, and the baby was not exactly wanted, there is a likelihood that if something happens to it, the parents will want another baby afterwards.

Dr G. commented:

I never refer my families for vasectomy until the baby's a year old, for this very reason. But if that system fails, and they would like another child, then I would put them in touch with the surgeon and say that in the tragic circumstances, would he consider reversing the operation – bearing in mind that there's a strong chance that the reversal will fail. That's a risk they have to take, but it's well worth while trying. But I would hope that by careful planning beforehand, they don't get into that situation.

Dr G. said that in theory, even a complete sterilization can sometimes be reversed, though in practice it is sometimes difficult or impossible. This was the risk you took when you were sterilized – that it could not necessarily be reversed.

Dr C. agreed that a vasectomy should not be carried out until the most recent baby was one year old. However, if the situation arose, where a reversal was needed, he would certainly give the maximum advice and help, though the success rate of the operation was only forty to fifty per cent.

Despite the odds, it does seem that there was no need for the extended battle that Maureen B. had to fight with her medical advisers, before her husband was finally able to have a reversal operation – which, in his case, was successful.

Risk of another cot death

Many mothers are more likely to be concerned about the
physical aspects of the next pregnancy – wishing to be assured
that their next baby will be healthy – rather than the emotional
aspects, feeling like me, rightly or wrongly, that they can handle
their own emotions.

It was helpful to Jane that the paediatrician, at one of their
first meetings, had taken the trouble to contact the obstetrician
and was able to reassure Jane that from a physical point of view
there was no reason why she shouldn't have another baby, if
that was what she wanted, and that there was no reason why
she and David should experience another cot death.

Lynne's doctor, too, had reassured her saying, 'Don't worry; it
won't ever happen again.'

Dr G. commented:

You start with a clean slate, of course. In spite of what you read in the
papers, it is extremely rare for more than one cot death to occur in a
family. Statistically, there is an increased risk of a second cot death, but
it's still extremely rare, and it's not one that's worth considering.

We're not going to stop the mother being excessively anxious during
pregnancy and for the first 'x' months of the child's life and the mother
must expect to feel that. We, as her doctors, must expect to attend her
more frequently, to see her more often in the surgery when the new
baby is born. It's bound to happen.

Some parents may wish to time the next pregnancy, so that the
baby is neither born at the same time as their dead child, nor at
the most high risk times of the year. Lynne and Paul tried to
ensure that their next baby was not born in the middle of
winter nor in the month when Andrew was born.

At the time when I contemplated my next pregnancy, though
I knew that there was a greater risk of cot death occurring
during the autumn and winter months (between October and
March), I wanted another baby so badly that I was prepared to
take a chance on having the baby whenever it came. Neither
was I concerned whether or not the baby would be born in the
same month as Amanda – which she eventually was, though I
was glad it was not on the same day.

Research has since revealed not only that there are seasonal
peaks and dips of cot deaths, but also that there is a definitely
increased risk of cot death to those babies born in particular
months. Professor Knight, in a graph of cot deaths occurring in
Copenhagen in one year, contained in his book, *Sudden Death in
Infancy*, shows more than twice as many cot deaths occurring in

babies born between August and December as those born from February to April.

In many areas, parents may be able to participate in the CONI (Care of Next Infant) Scheme, funded by the Foundation (see page 126) in which the Health Visitor calls every week and the baby is monitored with either a portable apnoea monitor or by regular weighing or both. This may help to reassure parents once the new baby has arrived.

Problems in pregnancy

Despite everything I have said concerning guilt about the possible mistakes parents made in the course of the pregnancy and babyhood of the dead baby, when it comes to the next pregnancy, I think that they should think positively on how to create a healthy pregnancy. Guilt, as I have said, is a destructive emotion, even a form of self-indulgence. Whatever else it does do, it does not do good! However, to think carefully about how to give the next baby a good start in life can only be positive.

Some of the mothers I spoke to had problems in the pregnancy preceding the cot death and some had found that their babies' birthweights were less than they would have expected. Jane was taken into hospital for a few days at six months and given injections, though Naomi was subsequently a full term baby. Maureen A.'s baby, Timothy, was born early, after thirty-six weeks, weighing just over six pounds, following a possible placental malfunction. Maureen B.'s baby, Michelle, was just over seven pounds, but this was lower than she would have expected, since her two preceding boys were heavier babies.

Some babies are small even in spite of being full term babies. Lynne's baby was a little over six pounds, but she tended to have small babies. Sue and Neville's baby son, Anthony, like my baby Amanda, was born a week after the expected day of arrival, and he weighed 6lb 1oz which was much smaller than their 7lb 12oz daughter. Sue had not been able to eat well during pregnancy, being very sick. She also had family problems, which involved a certain amount of rushing around.

I, on the other hand, had no idea why Amanda was only 5½lb at birth. I had been a smoker of between five and ten cigarettes a day and though I knew that babies might have a lower birth weight if their mother smoked (though I did not at that time realize that smoking in itself put them more at risk generally), I had never envisaged that a significant weight loss might occur, particularly as my son had been nearly seven pounds. I was extremely shocked at Amanda's appearance when she was first born, since she looked as though she had been starved in the womb. During my next pregnancy, I was tested for an abnormality in the placenta because it was suggested this might have been the case in the previous pregnancy, but no abnormality was found.

The next pregnancy

Midwife Mrs E. said that the midwife would be likely to be in contact with the mother fairly early in pregnancy and if it was helpful, might be able to come to the parents' home to talk to them about their worries.

Though it is not possible to say why some babies have low birth weights, nor is it possible to prevent some premature births, or other difficulties. I asked Dr G. what he would recommend to try to ensure as many advantages as possible to the next baby.

That's going a long way back. Pre-conception – preparation starts then. The mother's health should be good before she tries to conceive. She should stop taking drugs, stop drinking alcohol and, more important, she should stop smoking. You'd be surprised how many are unable to cut out all three. By drugs, I mean even things like aspirin and paracetomol. And by drinking, I mean one drink. And smoking – a lot of women do feel it's simpler to give up smoking before they conceive and for the rest of the pregnancy – and preferably for the rest of their lives for their own sake, but from the baby's point of view, for that pregnancy.

We've started in our practice what's called pre-conception sessions. My lady partner's doing this as part of Family Planning. The next stage on from contraception is planning for pregnancy. She talks about these things – proper diet, balanced vitamins. And that's part of the process of making yourself as healthy as possible for potential pregnancy. After that it's just ordinary common sense care.

Mrs E. confirmed that she too would like both parents to think about their health before conception. They should consider whether the husband was drinking and smoking, as well as the wife, whether the wife was working, and whether she had a stressful job. Should she consider giving it up earlier this time?

As little as three weeks into the pregnancy, you've got the nervous system beginning to be formulated and anything that interferes with that is going to have a permanent effect on that baby. That is why we have gone so much into the pre-conceptual idea, in that, in terms of smoking and alcohol, they're now saying that that also needs to be abstained from, at least two or three months before you plan to start a family. It has definitely been identified that smoking constricts the blood vessels that supply the baby, and this causes the baby to be small, because it does not get nourishment through the blood supply.

As far as alcohol was concerned, Mrs E. explained that doctors do not yet know what quantity of alcohol could be damaging for the unborn child, which is why they are recommending that pregnant women take none at all.

Mrs E. said that where a mother appeared to be carrying a low birthweight child, there would possibly be more frequent scanning to see if the cause could be identified. In some cases a stay in hospital might be advisable to see if complete bedrest might improve the situation.

I asked Dr C. about the possibility of placental malfunction, or poor function. I mentioned the test that I had had during my last pregnancy, which would have revealed such a malfunction. He pointed out that, in addition to this test, which might be carried out in some cases, nowadays a scan would also be likely to show whether or not a baby is 'small for dates'. If this is found to be the case, doctors can only advise the mother to be very, very careful. Like Dr G., Dr C. put emphasis on the pregnant woman giving up smoking and alcohol, particularly in such a case.

Rest as much as possible; good diet; avoid smoking; avoid alcohol. All the sensible things to build up your strength; and consequently, we hope that as much of your nutrition as possible is going to the placenta, rather than to burning up your energy.

Smoking

The subject of smoking is an emotive one for those people who would like to give it up and still cannot, even though they want to do the best for their baby. The fact that mothers are likely to be in a more tense state following the death of their previous baby means that they are likely to want to cling to this prop.

Jane had already cut down her smoking 'to almost nil' when she was expecting Naomi, but she found it very hard to do that when she was expecting James, partly because of her emotional state about being pregnant, and particularly because she had smoked very heavily after Naomi's death. She was terrified at all stages – terrified of miscarrying, terrified of anything going wrong.

Even the doctor said to me, 'Don't attempt to give up smoking, because *you* need it. The one thing you can't cope with on top of everything else is trying to give up smoking.'

But then of course, there were people saying, 'I would have thought that *you* of all people would know better than to smoke when you're pregnant.' And then I'd think, 'Oh, my God, what am I doing? I'm trying to kill this baby.' I think people could be very callous and cruel about that sort of thing. Because – as they said – I, of all people, knew. I didn't need *them* to keep telling me.

Lynne had given up smoking when she was expecting Andrew. She did not resume it until the day of the inquest, when another parent offered her a cigarette. However, when she found she was pregnant again, she gave it up.

No one pressured me to give up smoking, partly because links between smoking during pregnancy and various types of problems in babyhood were not established at that time. I was still smoking when I conceived and, initially, I merely tried to cut it down. However, I began to find that I was so consumed with shame, when I did smoke, that I might be taking the risk of producing another baby of low birth weight, that gradually I smoked less and less and finally not at all. My method was to delay the first cigarette of the day until later and later each day, and also to keep a record of how many cigarettes I had smoked each day. Just before giving up smoking completely, I got to a stage of having one each day, and then only four or five that week. Keeping such a record does give you a certain satisfaction. Even if you have not managed to give up smoking before, it will still be beneficial to the baby to give up smoking during the early part of pregnancy.

Alcohol

The recommendation to give up all alcohol is a fairly new idea. Maureen, who had had the odd glass of wine during previous pregnancies, did in fact cut out alcohol completely when she was expecting Julie.

Parents wishing to know more about pre-conceptual care and diet may wish to be in contact with an organization called Foresight, which is carrying out research into this subject.

9 The next baby

When the nine long months of waiting are over, there are still problems to be faced. I remember welcoming the birth of my daughter Karen with relief rather than with ecstatic happiness. I was aware that I must now face all the worries I had succeeded in putting to one side during the pregnancy. However, I was delighted that I had had a second daughter.

The 'wrong' sex

To an outsider, it might seem illogical that a parent can be concerned about a trivial matter like the sex of a baby, when one might imagine that the only concern would be that the baby was healthy. Nevertheless, it is difficult to put aside those preferences, particularly when the child that died was the only child of that sex in the family.

I had been hoping for a girl when Amanda was born, since I already had a son. Therefore, I desperately hoped for another girl when my next baby was expected. I did try to put those hopes out of my mind during the pregnancy, but I think I would have been extremely disappointed if I had had a boy. Possibly, I would then have considered yet another pregnancy.

However, Pam, who already had a son and a daughter, was not disappointed at having another daughter. She felt that when, after her son's death, a daughter had been born, it was almost as if a mistake had been rectified, because her husband had wanted a girl originally.

Lynne and Paul, who lost the second son of their family, did not want a replacement of their son, and Paul, in particular, would have preferred a daughter.

Jane felt that, in ordinary circumstances, families who desired a child of one sex and subsequently had a baby of the other sex were likely to be philosophical about it; but they were less likely to be so, if this happened after the loss of a baby. Nevertheless, because it was her *first* baby that had died, Jane felt at first it did not really matter what sex the second baby was, provided it survived the first year, but thought that it would possibly make more difference the next time and certainly, the time after. When James was very young, Jane was glad that he was a different sex from her first baby, because she would have felt even more worried if she had had a girl. Now that he is a toddler and the danger time has passed, she wishes he had been a girl, and she still would like to have a daughter.

Maureen A. tried very hard, before the next baby was born, to prepare herself for the possibility that she might have a daughter. She was disappointed when the midwife told her it was a girl, though she tried not to show it.

Because she was a very big baby, when she was all wrapped up and put in her cot, she looked more like Timothy had done when he'd died than when he'd been born, and I found that very upsetting. Then I think it probably took me the whole nine to ten weeks that had been his life-span to get used to her. She was a very lovable, cuddly baby, but I still kept thinking, 'This is part of the time that Timothy had,' and it was only when she got to about ten weeks that I could think that she was living her own life – a lifetime of her own. I think that about then, I got used to the idea, and by the time she was about six months old, I thought it was absolutely lovely to have a little girl.

Maureen who, at the time of speaking, was pregnant again, had mixed feelings about whether she wanted her expected child to be a boy, though she would have liked her older son to have had a little brother again, in spite of an eight year gap between them.

Sometimes when a child is born that is not the hoped-for sex, the mother worries less, superstitiously feeling that she was only destined to lose daughters, if she had a son after a daughter, or vice versa. These feelings are not linked to the statistics, which show a slightly greater risk to boy babies.

Maureen B. felt this way, and was not unduly worried about her son during the first few months of his life. He was a big baby, and she felt quite sure that nothing would happen to him. However, she felt that if she had had a girl, she might have been more worried. Once her husband Tony had had the reversal of his vasectomy carried out and Maureen became pregnant, she hoped very much that the new baby would be a girl. She found the birth of a third son instead of the hoped-for daughter 'devastating'. Sadly, she had not really adjusted to the birth of a son and although a couple of years had passed, she was still disappointed.

Naming the baby

It is not considered to be a good idea to name the baby after his or her dead sibling and none of the parents I spoke to reused their dead babies' names as first names. However, Maureen used names for her daughter Julie that she would have used if Timothy had been a girl. She commented:

This was something I was not entirely happy about. I did feel a bit uneasy about it – sort of superstitious. I kept thinking, 'Perhaps it is trying to bring him back; or perhaps giving some of the things that went wrong with him to her.' But in fact, I feel quite happy about it now. I was aware though that we consciously avoided the names which had been used by friends of ours who had a cot death.

I have never enquired whether it is also considered to be unwise to do what I did, that is, to use Amanda's name as a second name for my second daughter Karen. I have never regarded her as the same child returned to me, and in using the name Amanda I rather treated it as one more way of ensuring that my first daughter would be remembered – that, in fact, Karen would almost be the guardian of her memory.

Dealing with fear

Though Lynne did not regard herself as a worrier, her GP recommended that she have a word with the paediatrician in hospital, after Graham was born, to set her mind at rest. Lynne was annoyed to find that the paediatrician had checked over the baby in her absence when she was registering his birth. Lynne insisted that he return to discuss the baby with her personally, which he did. Subsequently, when Graham was three-and-a-half weeks old (the age when Andrew had died), she took him to her own GP, who gave him a thorough check-up and told her he was a very healthy baby. She therefore had a certain amount of confidence, and was not unduly afraid during the baby's first months.

The way I dealt with my fear was to put it into compartments. I managed to convince myself that nothing would happen during the first few weeks, since most cot deaths do not occur at that early stage. So it was only when Karen reached the age that Amanda had been at the time of her death that I began to be fearful. After that, it was a case of taking each day as it came, and being thankful and grateful that she had survived. Once she was about eight months old, which coincided with the beginning of summer, I finally felt she was safe. Maureen had similar feelings about her new baby: 'It was very worrying and I think that really it was just a question of getting through the days as best we could.'

I found that I had periodic panics at some trivial problem, but I always had easy access to the surgery and to the baby clinic where I saw both the doctor and Health Visitor. But in some respects, no professional could quell the sudden panics that sometimes occurred for no particular reason when I was on my own.

Extra support

Most parents are more nervous than they would otherwise be and welcome extra support from the Health Visitor. In the past this has not always taken place. Some mothers are regarded as experienced and in spite of the cot death have not received as many automatic calls as they would have liked, though the GP is usually understanding about extra visits to the practice, which are more likely to be instigated by the mother. The Foundation's CONI project hopes to provide the extra automatic support that has been lacking in the past.

Maureen A. did not receive many visits from her Health Visitor, but like me, found that the doctor would always make time for her at the surgery when she was worried, and she got the impression that he had expected to see a lot more of her.

In Maureen B.'s case, the Health Visitor who had been extremely helpful after Michelle's birth and death, had left the practice, and the new Health Visitor saw Maureen only once during the early months of her son's life, when the midwife passed mother and baby into her care. After that, she did not come at all. Maureen conceded that it was her fourth child, and perhaps from a practical point of view, she did not need guidance, but had she done so, it would not have been forthcoming. In addition, though she might have needed help on an emotional level, the only person who recognized that was the previous Health Visitor, who warned her husband that she would be disappointed at the birth of a son.

A little extra understanding is helpful in the hospital too. Lynne was disappointed that baby Graham's colouring was totally different from that of his brother, and in addition she was upset that he was not a girl. She became very upset when she got back to the ward a few hours after she had given birth and could not stop crying. The staff came to find out what was wrong and having heard about the cot death, they asked if she would like to cuddle the new baby and then drew the curtains round her and left her with him. Despite Lynne's initial reaction to her son, Graham took his rightful place in the family, and she felt that having another baby had been the right step for her to take. However, to a certain extent, she felt she was ignored during her stay in hospital, and was aware during her labour of staff whispering about the fact that she had had a cot death.

Any more children?

The birth and survival of a new baby does not necessarily make the mother very much more confident as far as a subsequent baby is concerned. Maureen A., in her fourth pregnancy, took the same precautions as before, and made arrangements to use an apnoea monitor for a second time. Jane has not had another baby after the birth of James, her surviving child. She told me:

Part of me heaves this enormous sigh of relief that he's safe now. And I'm steeling myself to go through it again, because I don't think it's going to be any easier. You have a fear – you think it's you – you're this jinx. It emanates from you somewhere deep down – 'You touch this child and it's going to die.' It's illogical. I don't feel: 'I've been through it now, and I know I can have a surviving child.' Possibly, it makes me even more nervous because I feel, 'I've got one; maybe my luck's running out. Maybe with the next one, I won't be so lucky.'

I also felt that once I had a son and daughter it would be asking too much to have any more children. Though, at times I felt that two children was a smaller family than I would have liked, perhaps partly because of the previous failed pregnancies, I felt I could not face pregnancy and birth again. In addition, the prospect of the various things that could go wrong could not altogether be put from my mind, and I was no longer spurred on by the desperate desire for another baby, as before.

Specific worries

Since many cot deaths seem to be associated with respiratory infections, it is not surprising if parents are unduly worried about colds.

Colds

Dr G. confirmed again:

Usually with a baby's snuffles, I will do nothing. I give advice on
supplying extra fluids, keeping baby not too hot – there's a strong
temptation in many households to overheat babies' rooms, and I
always tell them to steam the room. Very useful in relieving congestion
and catarrh. It doesn't cure the disease, but it makes the breathing
easier.

Since it is likely that there is an association between
respiratory infections and some cot deaths, it would be sensible
to avoid colds if one can. It is extremely difficult if there are
older toddlers in the family, but one can at least try to keep the
babies away from outsiders' infections, even at a cost of
occasionally seeming to be unsociable or overfussy.

Sleeping place and sleeping position

There has been periodic publicity about mattresses and carry-
cots, and parents may wonder in what position and where their
baby is most safe and comfortable.

Maureen A. said that she was quite pleased to get Julie out of
her carry-cot and into a big cot.

There was a sort of lingering thought – was it too enclosed in the
carry-cot, and also with the cot, I could see her more easily when I
opened the door to check her.

Timothy, her cot death baby had always lain on his stomach
with his face flat downwards, as his brother had done without
ill effect. Maureen tried putting Julie on her stomach, but
propped up sideways a little more, but it did not seem to work
with her any more than it had done with her brothers. If they
were on their sides, they invariably rolled on their backs, even
in spite of a rolled up nappy positioned on the mattress, and
then Maureen would be concerned at the possibility of them
choking, if they were left lying on their backs. She always tried
to put their heads to one side, but both boys put their faces
downwards. She used a safety mattress with ventilation holes.

Midwife, Mrs E., confirmed that she would recommend using
mattresses with large ventilation holes on top.

Despite using a safety mattress, I found myself unable to
place Karen on her stomach. Like Maureen, I could not rid
myself of vaguely uneasy feelings – in my case, about Amanda's

position in the cot – but in addition, I found it essential that I could see Karen's face, as soon as I went into the room.

The Foundation for the Study of Infant Deaths has stated that:

Very many babies throughout the UK sleep in the prone position (on their tummies) with no ill effect. Some recently published research, though, has suggested that sleeping on the tummy may have an association with cot death. This does not mean that sleeping prone has necessarily caused the death, rather that it may have been a contributory factor.

We still do not know the reasons for these findings. Overheating may also be a contributory factor in some cot deaths; and it is possible that young infants, especially if tightly swaddled, find it difficult to throw off their bedclothes when lying on the tummy if they become too hot. Once a baby is strong enough to turn over he or she will find the position in which they feel most comfortable. We hope that ongoing research will soon help us to understand other possible factors connected with sleeping position.

The Foundation now normally advises that parents adopt the traditional measure of lying babies on their sides.

Breast feeding

Maureen A. had not been very successful with breast feeding:

I had tried to breast feed Nicholas and I tried again with her [Julie], but she was rather half-hearted about it all, and I'm not one of these Jersey cows on two legs, so in the end I gave it up. I did persevere, but I gave it up in the end because the Health Visitor gave me scales, and I found that in fact I was only producing a quarter of what she should have had. I put her on the bottle, but then she hardly drank any more anyway; she had been such a whacking great baby to begin with that I think that probably she didn't need to eat much at first.

Maureen B. who had felt so guilty at not breast feeding Michelle, did feed her next baby. However, Jane, although she had had no trouble at all feeding Naomi, did have problems with breast feeding when her second baby, James, was born. In her case, however, she felt pressurized to continue breast feeding and was not at all convinced that this was a good thing.

Looking back, it was quite obvious that I was going to have trouble with James. It was a year almost to the day since Naomi had been born. I was in a very emotional state and very concerned about him. (The first month or six weeks is dreadful – it's a living hell.)

Despite the fact that James was not feeding well, even when Jane came out of hospital after three days, she continued to give James breast milk for four-and-a-half months, but during most of that period, she was expressing her milk, having hired an electric pump, and feeding it to him from a bottle. She felt she should have been told to stop and put James on to conventional bottle feeding. However, the fact that she was told over and over again, 'It's better for you to breast feed him; you must keep on trying', and the fact that she was not getting on very well made her very upset at the time and makes her feel rather cross now.

You are obviously very sensitive to what's best for this new baby. But, I'd like to think that they should have said to me after a week of totally unsuccessful breast feeding, 'Look, you're emotionally upset, anyway. It's obviously not going to work. . . Bottle feed him.'

I was perhaps fortunate in that I breast fed all three of my children successfully, though I had introduced solids in addition extremely early in Amanda's case. Successful breast feeding is sometimes a matter of having confidence that you have enough milk and it may be difficult to believe in yourself when you have lost faith in your ability as a mother. During my first pregnancy, I obtained a copy of the National Childbirth Trust leaflet on breast feeding, which I found very helpful and, in addition, I ordered a nursing bra from them, which I also wore for support during the last month or so of pregnancy. During the night-time feeds, I kept a flask of milky cocoa by my bedside. I am an advocate of breast feeding where possible, and I was delighted to be able to continue breast feeding my second daughter until she was eight months old.

Miss S., Health Visitor, suggested that if the milk supply seemed inadequate, it might be helpful to offer a bottle after, but not instead of the breast feed, particularly at the end of the day, when the mother is tired.

The National Childbirth Trust currently produces a leaflet called 'Thinking about Breast Feeding', and nursing bras can be ordered in advance of the birth, by sending measurements, together with a cheque. The bras can also be worn during the last couple of months of pregnancy, when additional support is helpful. Their address is included with other useful addresses, at the back of the book.

Mixed feeding

Both doctors seemed to agree that ideas on weaning babies off milk and on to 'solid' foods go through fashions. Dr C. recommended:

The current feeling is that it's milk of some description, preferably breast, but otherwise a good bottle feed till three months, then gradually increase solids over the next three months, then drop the bottle altogether and take normal cow's milk, increasing the solids and decreasing the milk, as the year goes by. There's no definite rule. That's a generalization. I think I'm of the school that believes milk is very good food value and I would hold back solids, just because it's more convenient with a bottle. But when you've got a hungry baby that doesn't settle at night, you're desperate to do something, so give it a bit of baby rice, or something like that, just to fill the baby up a bit. But try to avoid it before three months, is the general thinking at the moment, though that may change in the next five years. Things have a habit of changing.

Maureen A. was concerned about introducing solids, even though Timothy had not had them and she managed to avoid giving them to Julie until she was about fourteen weeks old. However, at this stage, Julie was not gaining much weight, and the Health Visitor persuaded Maureen that she should introduce solids, since this was a time of rapid growth, including brain development.

Overheating

As mentioned earlier, it is now considered that overheating may be a contributory factor in some cot deaths, and it is therefore a source of concern to doctors and midwives alike.

Sometimes when a mother has left hospital, and returned to the normality of her home, she can become over-anxious about keeping the baby warm. The hospital nursery is often an excessively warm room, since it is catering for tiny newborn babies whose 'heat-controlling mechanism' may not yet be working properly. It balances this out by keeping less vulnerable babies in lighter clothing. However, the mother may be tempted to have extra clothing (e.g. vest plus nightie plus cardigan plus sleeping suit, etc.) and blankets, as well as keeping the room warm. In addition, large cot blankets are sometimes folded to fit the carry cot, thus creating several thicknesses. Midwife, Mrs E. said that where they found that babies were too wrapped up, they were now telling mothers to turn their heating down.

As long as the temperature doesn't drop below 65°F (18°C), then you should be perfectly all right, and after about a week, there's no need to keep the heating on all night, because the houses, these days, are so well insulated that the heat you've had on during the evening is sufficient to go through the night, except in exceptional weather conditions.

Mrs E. said that only in houses which were not centrally heated was there likely to be any concern about keeping the baby warm enough, and in addition, she stressed they were no longer recommending the tight swaddling of babies that used to occur.

Experts recommend that in a normally heated house, the baby should be covered, as you would cover yourself, with two or three correctly sized blankets. Young babies' ability to cool themselves may not be well developed and they may suffer from heat stress before showing signs of stress or dealing with it by sweating. If babies are suffering from an infection, their ability to deal with heat stress may be even more impaired, and this may be the occasion when they are even more heavily wrapped by anxious parents.

If parents are in a draughty house without heating, they might consider buying a thermostatic electric plug. An electric convector heater could be plugged into this and it would automatically switch itself on and off, according to the position of the thermostatic plug.

It is important to remember to dress the baby more warmly when he is going out in the cold, than when he is in the house. In addition, in the borderline times of year when winter merges with spring or autumn, and heating may be off one day and on the next, the baby's clothing and covering should be adjusted accordingly.

Moments of panic

I often accidentally awoke Karen just before I went to bed, by touching her just to make sure she was all right. She was an extremely light sleeper and, as a result of that, she had quite a lot of extra late-night feeds.

Marian, like me, experienced moments of panic. Nicholas was very fair, and when he was asleep he looked pale, and she too would touch him in his sleep to make sure all was well. However, in spite of the panics, she felt she would not have wanted to have an apnoea monitor. She said:

We had told the children that it didn't happen twice, and therefore, if the baby came out of hospital with all these contraptions, they'd think, 'Well, is it going to happen again?' and they'd be worried, so we tried to keep things as normal as possible.

Care of Next Infant (CONI) Programme

Though parents hope that they can bring up the new baby as normally as possible, most still feel the need for additional support. In areas where the Foundation has been able to set up a CONI scheme, parents are offered support which will automatically include regular weekly contact with the Health Visitor, the completing of symptom diaries and at regular intervals, Sheffield weight charts. The scheme would also include the provision of apnoea monitors, *daily* weighing and measurement of environmental temperatures, if parents required any or all of these facilities. In addition, parents would have support from a knowledgeable GP and ready access to a paediatrician involved with the programme. The involvement of all professionals in the scheme would commence in pregnancy and continue until the baby was beyond the cot death period.

The CONI programme has grown out of the knowledge obtained and reactions of participants in the earlier Infant Home Surveillance Research Projects funded by the Foundation.

Infant Home Surveillance Research Project

In 1980, the Foundation funded the Infant Home Surveillance Research Project to provide and evaluate support for families who had a subsequent child after a cot death. Firstly, the project undertook a pilot study of 100 families, who were randomly allocated an apnoea monitor or weighing scales and Sheffield centile weighing charts for daily weighing. All parents completed a daily record of symptoms of illness and the Health Visitor visited all parents weekly, and filled in the centile weight charts for those infants being weighed regularly. In 1984, the project became a multicentre study and between 1984 and 1988, the number of centres involved expanded from 5 to 23, covering about a tenth of the country's health areas.

Jane, who was involved in the pilot scheme, felt the surveillance scheme would be very valuable to any mother who was worried about her next baby. The regular visits from the Health Visitor, and the ability to keep a check on details of the baby's general health through the weighing charts, were very reassuring to her.

Dr G. also commented that he thought the surveillance system for the next baby would be very useful.

I think informally we do this anyway. Automatically, everybody pays more attention to the next baby. The advantage of the scheme is that you've got a set of fixed guidelines to look for.

Lynne would have welcomed the opportunity of being involved in a home surveillance scheme, particularly since she would have found it reassuring to have had more visits from the Health Visitor.

Ideally, the Foundation would wish to interest all health authorities in participating in a CONI scheme, to provide country-wide organised support for all cot death parents.

Though almost unanimous in their desire for the type of automatic support provided by a Home Surveillance Project, parents' feelings about apnoea monitors vary considerably.

Apnoea monitors

Apnoea monitors did not exist at the time when Amanda died, but over the years they have become increasingly sophisticated and less expensive. Some mothers desperately feel the need for a monitor when their next baby is born, while others feel equally strongly that to have one and to live with the occasional false alarms would make them very uneasy.

Modern alarms are light-weight and battery operated, usually giving a visual and sound signal if regular breathing movements have ceased for longer than a pre-set time of ten or twenty seconds. Some mothers have found the monitor's regular tick or bleep, when the baby is breathing normally, very reassuring, and without them would feel the need to hover over the baby all day and night. However, apnoea monitors have their disadvantages. Although they warn of the cessation of breathing movements, it is possible for a baby to have a blocked airway, which is not immediately detected, since the muscles controlling breathing movements can continue for a time, even though no air is reaching the lungs.

Cot death parents have not in the past and still do not automatically receive an apnoea alarm to monitor their next baby. Though their capacity to reassure some parents is great, their ability to save a child's life is uncertain and their value to a parent, if unsupervised, is also more doubtful. Some parents in areas which participated in the Foundation Infant Home Surveillance Research Project were randomly allocated an alarm, and those parents now in a CONI scheme are offered one as a matter of course. Other parents who, despite the monitors' limitations, particularly wish to use one, sometimes buy or find other ways of obtaining them. In some cases, parents raise funds to obtain a monitor for their local hospital, to be loaned out.

Maureen, who was extremely anxious to have a monitor, but

who at that time was unable to participate in a Foundation scheme, managed to borrow one.

Some monitors are taped to the baby's abdomen and can be worn in almost every situation, but Julie's monitor was a flat sensor which went underneath the mattress, so that it was not actually wired to her body. Though she was monitored whenever she was in her cot or pram, Maureen did not find it intrusive, and it was not affected by her moving around until she was about nine and a half to ten months old.

A few times she lifted herself up, off the mattress when she was awake early in the morning and it started to 'beep' and we rushed in, but at that point, I think, the fear had gone. Even though we knew that in theory it could go on for longer, I think at that stage we were fairly confident that she was going to reach her first birthday.

Sue attended a meeting of several cot death mothers, at which one mother had an apnoea monitor. Whilst looking at it, the timer device got mis-set and it went off shortly afterwards. For a moment, the twenty mothers sat paralysed with fear. Sue felt that if she had had another baby, she would have found it difficult to cope with such false alarms.

I do not think I would have wished to use an apnoea alarm, had it been available when I had my next baby, and in fact I even turned down the baby alarm at night, so that I was not tempted to listen for every breath. Dr G's reservations about the apnoea alarm summed up my own feelings.

It can concentrate attention on just one aspect of the child – this is presumably offered to the next child along – and that child really ought to have as normal an upbringing as possible. It should not be treated as if it were in cotton wool, cosseted. It's an ordinary healthy child, you presume, and so the person using the apnoea alarm must recognise that the child has to be allowed a normal life – to be able to go to sleep, wake up, cry, breathe irregularly, go out in the fresh air – all the sorts of things that ordinary babies are allowed to do; and the effect of continually monitoring a child's every breath, which is literally what you're doing, can, I think, be very wearing.

Midwife, Mrs. E. was anxious to remind parents that it was no use having an apnoea monitor, unless they had learned how to resuscitate the baby, in the event of it ceasing to breathe. However, once parents understood that, and were confident of their ability to do that, they might find it reassuring.

Parents who receive a monitor as part of a CONI scheme will

at the same time receive the support and supervision necessary for its correct operation.

Is it worth going through the fears and panics? I would have thought that if you can face the other problems, then fear alone should not put you off having another baby. For me, the birth of Karen, after all my previous sadnesses, was the start of a period of great happiness, which more than made up for the fear.

Mandy sums it up:

I don't think it is right for me to tell people to have another child. I say it was right for me and was the start of my looking forward instead of back, but they must make the decision themselves.

10 Looking back

Making progress

In the years since I lost baby Amanda there has been a
tremendous increase in understanding and information about
cot death, so that I do not feel that parents today have to
endure quite the same feelings of isolation as parents in the
days before the existence of the British Guild for Sudden Infant
Death Study and the Foundation for the Study of Infant Deaths.
The Foundation, which came into being after the grandmother
of a baby who had died provided money for a major seminar in
Cambridge in 1970, eventually embraced the British Guild and
now has a network of parent groups throughout the British Isles
and links with similar groups in other countries in the Western
world. Not only are increased funds raised each year which
enable more and more research projects to be undertaken, but
as a result of the increase in publicity, more bereaved parents
are made aware of the Foundation, and its local groups.

It is sad that occasionally the efforts of the many who work so
hard in fund-raising, in research, in spreading information and
in reassuring bereaved parents, have been marred by the
periodic appearances of misguided statements or distorted
reports in the media. Parents may find it difficult not to be hurt
by these unfortunate articles, which are often full of
generalizations and uncertainties. In Newsletter No. 26 (August
1984) the Foundation set out guidelines on how to read and
interpret such articles. This is an emotive subject and so I have
reproduced the newsletter article in full.

Cot death and publicity

Increased publicity about cot deaths has highlighted the

strength of public feeling about the scale of the cot death problem, the anguish these tragedies bring to bereaved families and the anxiety felt by young parents today.

Because the reasons for the unexplained deaths are unknown, many people put forward theories which can be very upsetting. Some reports which appear in the media are misleading, inaccurate or capable of misinterpretation.

The following is adapted from advice prepared by Dr John Maloney, Monash University, and is reprinted by courtesy of the Sudden Infant Death Research Foundation, Australia.

How to evaluate media reports on 'cot death'

Ignore the headlines – often they do not accurately describe the article/contents.

Read the text and underline the words 'might'. 'may', 'possibly', 'could' . . . this helps to emphasize any uncertainties in the report.

Re-read the text – Then ask yourself these questions:

- *Are the deaths sudden, unexpected, and without adequate explanation?* Is the report consistent with the definition of SIDS? or *Are the deaths sudden but explained deaths?*
- *Does it take into account that sudden unexplained infant deaths occurred in earlier centuries and that the rate has changed little over the years?*
  This means that suggested theories relating to modern technology or recent changes in child care practice are unlikely to hold the key or provide the clue to the majority of unexplained deaths.
- *Is the article based on an idea that has not yet been tested?* Have experiments not yet been performed?
- *Is the article a report of a random observation?* Have they seen only one or just a few cases? Does it need further work to establish a hypothesis?

Remember

- The scientist may not have said what is reported.
- The need for over-simplification may lead to the wrong impression.
- The interest of the scientist may have been in another area. It may have been the journalist who asked about a possible relationship to cot death which led to it becoming a headline.

The Foundation has also produced information in the form of leaflets, check lists, video cassettes and films for health professionals, the police and the public. However, in spite of the information available, some professionals should ask themselves if they could improve on the way they have helped us. So many of the parents I spoke to received excellent help that I have no desire to carp, but our medical advisers could bear in mind that they must learn to put aside their own feelings of having failed or feeling guilty, if they are to help us. We need their support and their presence. We don't want them to make the same mistake as others and leave us in isolation to face our tragedy.

Obsessions

We may be left with strange obsessions which are more superstitious than logical. Sue and Neville had been eating a particular brand of boxed chocolates during the evening when Anthony was discovered. Even now Sue is upset by people offering them to her and has never bought them since. Similarly, I was making an unusual recipe the night of Amanda's death, and I have never cooked that dish again. I am also obsessive about waste; I find that I collect and hoard all sorts of things that may be useful at some time, and feel quite guilty at throwing them away when the clutter becomes too great. I often remember my feelings at the time of Amanda's death – that the year since the beginning of that pregnancy had been 'wasted', that her life had been 'wasted' – and I wonder whether this is linked to this obsession.

Ways of remembering

Apart from the amount of time and effort put into emotional memorials, people vary in their feelings towards the baby's actual resting place and more conventional remembrances. Pam, for example, did not want to know where her baby's ashes were scattered and has only visited the Garden of Remembrance recently, after many years whereas Marian goes quite often to her baby's grave. Pam, through the support group which she runs, knows of other mothers, who being quite close to the churchyard or cemetery where the babies were buried, have even gone daily for a while, whilst others simply could not face it. Once again, this is a choice for each individual.

In the Jewish religion, it is usual to have a burial, rather than a cremation, but the cemetery where Amanda is buried is a long way from where we live. Michael and I go there about once a year to visit Amanda's grave, which is in a small plot devoted exclusively to babies and children. Another tradition which we observe is to light a memorial candle on the anniversary of her death, which burns for a full day.

Mandy wrote to me:

In our house, we talk of Sophie, her picture hangs on the wall and the children think of her as an unseen sister. I would feel very guilty pretending that she had not existed; she did and we loved her very much and we remember her birthday and Christmas with a special arrangement of flowers for the table.

Maureen B. said that she still thinks of Michelle quite a lot, though not necessarily in a desperately sad way. The children talk about their sister, and the family keep a photograph of her in the room.

Maureen A., who kept her photographs of Timothy in the family album, regretted now that they did not have more. However, Neville had other thoughts about photographs:

'. . . your memories of the baby aren't in a photograph; what we still remember about Anthony can't be transmitted on to a bit of film'.

As time has passed, dates which were once, for me, exclusively Amanda's birth and death anniversaries have held other events, so that they have a happy as well as a sad significance. The birth of my only niece occurred on the ninth anniversary of Amanda's birthday, a very moving and emotional day for me.

Jane felt there was a conflict in her emotions.

He [James] is wonderful and to us, he's a joy. But I don't think you can ever take it away. I'd like to go back to before it happened and have it not happen. But, it's very difficult because it's all contradictions and complexities. I am a better person from what happened. I think I've gained more by it happening than I ever would have done by it not happening. I'm certainly a better mother than I would have been to Naomi. Without any question of doubt. And David as well, who hasn't entered into this conversation very much at all, is certainly a much better, more active, more involved father than he ever would have been to Naomi.

I find it very difficult – you think if people say to you, 'If you had one wish, what would it be?', the logical thing would be that I still had Naomi and it wouldn't have happened, but then, if I still had her, I wouldn't have him.

I find that that's almost the hardest thing to cope with – the fact that

I have gone forward and I can't have her back, and the worst thing in the world is that, being blatantly honest, I couldn't want her back. I find that I do resent that; it makes me bitter that I have to say that – normally, you don't have to deny any of your children.

I also find it very difficult now, when people say to you, 'Is it your first?', not to take the easy way out and just say, 'Yes'. Not because I want to deny her, because in my own little world, I don't. We keep photographs of her. We've got photographs around the house. When James gets old enough to understand anything, if he asks, he had a sister who died before he was born. We loved her just as much as we love him.

Sue, who had not had another baby said that whilst you do not necessarily 'get over' a death, your life goes on without that dead person. You spent the first two or three years looking back to the death, particularly in the first year; and then it became easier. She did regret not having a larger family, but she did not know that she regretted not having another baby. She had no idea now what life would be like if the baby had lived, but she was happy with her life the way it was. She added that her mother used to look in prams and say, 'My grandson should be that size now', but Sue said she never did that, though Neville commented that he still did it. However, Sue, running the 'new mothers' coffee morning each term at the local primary school, found herself realizing that a particular intake would have been Anthony's. Neville said that while no one suggested you should ever forget the dead child, you come to terms with your memories and you accept it.

Pam felt that the experience and the work she had done in her support group had given her confidence in her ability to deal with life and various situations. She felt able now to go to a function on her own, and confident enough to engage the nearest stranger in conversation. Pam said that at the time of Nicholas's death she thought she would never be the same again; perhaps that was right, perhaps she was not after all the same person. But she had thought that she would never get over it and she had got over it. Possibly, she was happier now, because she had learned to value happiness.

Marian found, as a nurse, that since the death of Victoria it was very much easier to talk to patients about dying. Previously, she had felt it was slightly arrogant to give advice to those who were dying, with no experience of how she would cope in such circumstances. 'I would quite happily make people cups of tea in the middle of the night and talk about anything else, other than what mattered to them, because I was scared of dying, but now I can talk about death.' Marian described how she was able to help in the case of a woman who was dying, but whose husband would not acknowledge the fact. Without necessarily mentioning her own tragedy, Marian had the confidence to mediate between husband and wife. In a similar vein, Pam felt that one naturally became a good listener and sometimes became the recipient of a variety of problems, unconnected with cot death.

But for some, the sadness remained.

Alice regarded the whole idea of consolation in the form of being strengthened as very offensive. She had no further children after the death of her baby and regarded her baby's short life and death as an experience very precious and very private, to be shared only with her immediate family. She explained to me that this was all she had of her baby and she did not want to lose it, either by talking or writing of it.

Maureen A. said that she had found no consolation. It was simply too dreadful.

Maureen B. said:

There'll always be that disappointment. Somehow, I don't think you really get over it; you learn to live with it. But it does get better.

My own feelings

After Amanda's death, I learned for the first time what real sorrow was, and after Karen's birth I discovered real happiness. The fact that I had coped with my ordeal caused me to be aware of strengths within myself of which I had previously been unaware, and this, in itself, gave me confidence to get involved in all sorts of activities which I would not have done previously.

In the course of time, I began to feel, partly because of these beneficial changes in my personality, that I could not regret the death any longer. I know that this feeling is one which is not shared by many people and in fact some mothers like Alice, as I mentioned above, have felt quite hurt or angered by me saying this. However, I must stress that I do not say it in any self-righteous way, nor imply that others should feel the same way. I am merely describing the changes that took place in my own feelings during the next few years.

The fact that I had 'replaced' the daughter I lost did, I feel sure, contribute to these feelings. Though I occasionally took note of what little girls of Amanda's age were doing in their lives, Karen was so close behind them that I did not feel I was missing out on a particular experience. If I had not had another daughter, there would, I believe, have been a feeling of permanent amputation of a part of me, from which I would never have completely recovered. But because I had the son and daughter I desired, I was satisfied with my children. In addition, the long wait for a longed-for second child meant that the birth of Karen brought me a particularly ecstatic happiness. If Amanda had not died, Karen would not have been born. Even if I had had another child subsequently, she would not have been Karen. And I would not have experienced the joy of that special baby, which was as a direct result of all the past sadness. I accepted my own apparent disloyalty to Amanda as a fact of life, at the same time never forgetting my pledge to continue to build my memorial to her in my own particular way.

In time, the intensity of my feelings faded; the ecstatic happiness subsided, just as the grief had done before. The certainty of God's presence faded and I suppose, to a certain extent, life returned to the black-and-white normality of the days prior to the birth of both babies.

When those feelings had left me, there was a new sadness at their passing and sometimes even a new guilt and a sense of disloyalty at the fact that there was no longer any pain. But at the same time, so much of my life since Amanda's birth and death has been affected by those events, that in a way I feel she is now irrevocably a part of me, just as she was before she was born.

I described this book as a journey *towards* recovery. As you can see, not everyone feels that they have made, or will ever make, a complete recovery. And certainly, no one who has experienced the tragedy of cot death can fail to be unchanged by it. Whether you feel you have been scarred or strengthened, you will in the end be a different person from the person you once were. You may feel you have lost your faith in yourself or in life itself; you may feel you have lost all your confidence, and although you may regain that confidence you will almost certainly have lost forever the naïve innocent belief that you were in some way invulnerable – immune to tragedy.

But in spite of this, you can be sure that the worst and most painful days will pass, the horror and shock of discovery will fade from the memory, and it will be possible to live again a life that contains laughter and happiness.

Appendix I
Check-list for GPs

The following check-list is produced by the Foundation for the Study of Infant Deaths to advise doctors how to help families coping with unexpected infant death.

Unexpected infant death - cot death - GP support of the family

One baby in every 500 live births dies unexpectedly for no obvious reason between the ages of 1 week and 2 years, 90% before 8 months. Although such tragedies are comparatively rare, in a group practice of 2 or 3 doctors a cot death is likely to occur every 2 to 4 years. A GP may be called to the home or the baby rushed to the surgery: often the baby is taken direct to a hospital casualty department. GPs should ensure in advance that coroners, hospitals and medical deputising services would inform the family doctor immediately of an unexpected infant death.

The following notes are intended to help doctors managing a cot death for the first time.

1 As soon as you hear of the baby's death, *contact the family* to express sympathy, by a home visit if possible. Early support prevents later misunderstandings.
2 Unless there is obvious injury, a history of illness or the parental attitude arouses suspicion, tell the parents it appears to be a cot death but that a *post mortem* examination will be necessary to establish the cause of death. If death remains unexplained, it may be registered as sudden infant death syndrome. Some parents want to see or hold their child after

death is confirmed but before the body is taken to a
mortuary.

3 Explain the *coroner's duty*, the possibility of an inquest, and
warn parents that they or relatives may be asked to identify
the body. Advise the parents that they will be asked to make
a statement to the coroner's officer or police, and that
bedding may be taken for examination to help establish the
cause of death. If necessary, give advice on registering the
death and making funeral arrangements. Coroner's officer
may need to know parents' choice of burial or cremation.

4 If considering offering parents a drug to alleviate the initial
shock, it is known that many do not want anxiolytics or anti-
depressants, but prefer something to *induce sleep*.

5 If the mother was *breastfeeding*, give advice on suppression of
lactation: prescribe medication and advise her to leave the
breasts alone except to express them once a day if an easy
method is available.

6 Take particular note of *siblings*. Remember that twin babies
carry extra risk of cot death and that a surviving twin may
need hospitalization for observation. Give guidance on
emotional needs of siblings, who may be neglected or over
protected; reassure parents that older children are not at
risk.

7 Advise parents of likely *grief reactions* such as aching arms,
hearing the baby cry, distressing dreams, and strong positive
or negative sexual feelings, but reassure them that these and
other symptoms such as loss of appetite and sleeplessness
are normal and temporary. Anger, sometimes directed
towards the GP, guilt and self-blame, especially on the part
of the mother, are common grief reactions for which the
doctor should be prepared.

8 Offer parents copies of the leaflet INFORMATION FOR THE
PARENTS FOLLOWING THE SUDDEN AND
UNEXPECTED DEATH OF THEIR BABY and the address of
the FOUNDATION FOR THE STUDY OF INFANT
DEATHS, 14–15 Belgrave Square, London SW1X 8PS;
telephone 01–235 1721. In addition to sponsoring medical
research, the Foundation offers further support and
information, and can put parents in touch with others who
have previously suffered a similar bereavement.

9 Make sure that parents have a *relative or close friend* very near
them during the 48 hours after the death, and offer
explanation to them and to the minister of religion. Make
sure the family's health visitor and other members of the

primary care team know of the baby's death and are
prepared to give continued support.
10 Arrange a subsequent meeting with the parents to *discuss the
cause of death*. Make sure the coroner informs you of the
initial and final post-mortem findings and consult with the
pathologist if any clarification is needed.
11 Offer parents a *later interview with a paediatrician* both for
themselves and the siblings. An independent opinion is
mutually beneficial to the parents and GP, restoring parental
confidence in the primary care team and sharing some of the
load of counselling particularly concerning future children.
12 Parents who have lost a baby unexpectedly will need extra
attention and support with their *subsequent children* from
their obstetrician, paediatrician, general practitioner and
health visitor.

Appendix II
Helping bereaved parents – do's and don't's

Prepared for the Compassionate Friends by: Lee Schmidt
                                            Parent Bereavement
                                            Outreach
                                            Santa Monica,
                                            California.

DO's		DON'T's	
—DO	let your genuine concern and caring show.	—DON'T	let your own sense of helplessness keep you from reaching out to a bereaved parent.
—DO	be available . . . to listen, to run errands, to help with the other children, or whatever else seems needed at the time.	—DON'T	avoid them because you are uncomfortable (being avoided by friends adds pain to an already intolerably painful experience).
—DO	say you are sorry about what happened to their child and about their pain.	—DON'T	say how you know how they feel (unless you've lost a child yourself you probably don't know how they feel).
—DO	allow them to express as much grief as they are feeling at the moment and are willing to share.	—DON'T	say 'you ought to be feeling better by now' or anything else which implies a judgement about their feelings.
—DO	encourage them to be patient with themselves,	—DON'T	tell them what they *should* feel or do.

not to expect too much of themselves and not to impose any 'shoulds' on themselves.

—DO allow them to talk about the child they have lost as much and as often as they want to.

—DON'T change the subject when they mention their dead child.

—DO talk about the special endearing qualities of the child they've lost.

—DON'T avoid mentioning the child's name out of fear of reminding them of their pain (they haven't forgotten it!)

—DO give special attention to the child's brothers and sisters – at the funeral and in the months to come (they too are hurt and confused and in need of attention which their parents may not be able to give at this time).

—DON'T try to find something positive (e.g. a moral lesson, closer family ties, etc.) about the child's death.

—DO reassure them that they did everything that they could, that the medical care their child received was the best or whatever else you know to be *true and positive* about the care given their child.

—DON'T point out at least they have their other children (children are not interchangeable; they cannot replace each other).

—DON'T say that they can always have another child (even if they wanted to and could another child would not replace the child they've lost).

—DON'T suggest that they should be grateful for their other children (grief over the loss of one child does not discount parent's love and appreciation of their living children.)

—DON'T make any comments which in any way suggest that the care given their child at home, in the emergency departments, hospital, or wherever was inadequate (parents are plagued by feelings of doubt and guilt without any help from their family and friends).

APPENDIX III
When to consult a doctor about your baby

The following leaflet is issued by the Foundation for the Study of Infant Deaths.

- IF YOU THINK your baby is ill even without any obvious symptoms CONTACT YOUR DOCTOR
- IF YOUR BABY shows any of the following symptoms especially if he has more than one YOUR DOCTOR would expect you to ask for advice.

Always urgent
- a fit or convulsion, or turns blue or very pale
- quick, difficult or grunting breathing
- exceptionally hard to wake or unusually drowsy or does not seem to know you

Sometimes serious
- croup or a hoarse cough with noisy breathing
- cannot breathe freely through his nose
- cries in an unusual way or for an unusually long time or you think your baby is in severe pain
- refuses feeds repeatedly, especially if unusually quiet
- vomits repeatedly
- frequently loose motions especially if watery (diarrhoea)
  Vomiting and diarrhoea together can lead to excessive loss of fluid from the body and this may need urgent treatment
- unusually hot or cold or floppy

- Even if you have consulted a doctor, health visitor or nurse, IF BABY is not improving or is getting worse, TELL YOUR DOCTOR AGAIN THE SAME DAY.

Emergency action

GET MEDICAL HELP IMMEDIATELY

- contact your DOCTOR
- telephone for an AMBULANCE (dial 999) or
- take baby to a Hospital ACCIDENT or CASUALTY department

While waiting for a doctor or ambulance to arrive:

If baby is not breathing

- stimulate baby by flicking the soles of his feet or picking him up. If no response, begin RESUSCITATION through his mouth-and-nose
- place baby on his back on a table or other firm surface
- suck the baby's nose clear

If baby does not gasp or breathe:

- support the back of his neck, tilt his head backwards and hold his chin upwards
- open your mouth wide and breathe in
- seal your lips round his nose and mouth
- breathe *GENTLY* into his lungs until his chest rises
- remove your mouth to allow the air to come out and let his chest fall
- repeat gentle inflations a little faster than your normal breathing rate, removing your mouth after each breath. *Baby should begin to breathe within a minute or so*

For a fit or convulsion

- lay your baby on his tummy with his head low and turned to one side.
- clear his mouth and nose of any sick or froth
- if he is hot, cool by sponging his head with tepid water (just warm)

For a burn or scald

- put the burnt or scalded part immediately in clean cold water
- lightly cover the part with a very clean cloth or sterile dressing
- do not apply oil or ointments; do not prick blisters

For an accident

- give FIRST AID if you know how
- if your baby has swallowed pills, medicines or household liquids, *take the bottle to the hospital as well.*

INFANT CARE GUIDANCE

Feeding

Breast feeding is the natural and the best way to feed your baby. Coughs, colds and tummy upsets are less frequent in breast-fed babies because breast milk helps them to resist and recover from infection. The early months of breast feeding are the most valuable. You and your baby will succeed best if you are quiet and undisturbed when feeding.

If you cannot breast feed or if you decide at some time to change to bottle feeding, keep the bottles and teats sterilized. Use a recommended baby milk up to the age of 6 months. Follow the instructions for making up the feeds accurately and carefully. If your bottle-fed baby appears hungry, the amount given at each feed and/or the number of feeds can be increased, but do not strengthen the mixture by adding extra milk powder. Never leave a baby sucking at his bottle on his own. Very few babies need solid foods before the age of 3 months, but most want a mixed diet as well as milk feeds by the age of 6 months. Consult your health visitor or doctor about feeding and vitamin supplements.

Babies aged over 1 month are sometimes thirsty and want a drink of water (without sugar), which has been boiled once only and cooled. This is especially important if they are feverish or have a cold, a chest infection, diarrhoea or vomiting. Illness is hardly ever caused by teething.

Crying

All healthy babies cry from time to time; some babies cry much more than others; and some babies cry regularly at a certain time of day. If crying continues and is not due to the usual causes – hunger, thirst, discomfort, wet or soiled nappies, tiredness, loneliness or being too hot or cold – and gentle rocking of the pram or cot or cuddling does not settle the baby, then see your doctor or health visitor.

Sleeping position

Select a cot with a firm, well-fitting mattress; a baby does not need a pillow. Traditionally newborn babies were put on their side to sleep with the lower elbow a little in front of the body, and put down on the opposite side after the next feed; this is still good practice. A rolled nappy placed by the back will prevent the baby rolling onto his back. Some babies like to sleep on their tummy, with the face turned to one side. As the baby grows the position in which he or she settles happily is probably the best.

Temperature

Keep your young baby's room at an even temperature of about 65°F (19°C) both day and night. Newborn babies need to be well wrapped until about one month old after which they are better at keeping themselves warm. Protect your baby including his head from draughts and use the pram hood in chill winds. In cold weather a baby can lose heat quickly even in his cot or pram. To check whether your baby is warm enough put your hand beneath the covers to feel his body. If the room is too warm or the baby overclothed, a baby can get too hot; he will feel hot or sweaty to touch and may be thirsty. Fresh air is good for a healthy baby, but not when he has a cold, or in foggy or cold weather. In hot weather keep the pram hood down and shade your sleeping baby from direct sunlight with a sun canopy.

Useful addresses

England

Foundation for the Study of Infant Deaths
(Cot Death Research and Support)
15 Belgrave Square
London SW1X 8PS
Tel: (01) 235 1721/235 0965
Registered charity no. 262191

Leaflets:
Information for Parents following the Sudden and Unexpected
    Death of their Baby
Your Next Child
When to Consult a Doctor About Your Baby
GP Check List
Guidelines for Accident and Emergency Departments
    (Reference list of articles)

Support for Parents
Appeals
Questions and Answers
Guidelines for Befrienders
Twice yearly Newsletter

Videos (VHS and Betamax):
After Our Baby Died
You are Not Alone
A Call for Help
My Beautiful Baby is Dead
I'm Sorry Your Baby is Dead but I Can't Tell You Why

Compassionate Friends
(An international organisation of bereaved parents offering
friendship and understanding to other bereaved parents)
National Secretary: Mrs Jillian Tallon
6 Denmark Street
Clifton
Bristol BS1 5DQ
Tel: (0272) 292778
Registered charity no. 263463

Leaflets:
No Death So Sad
Bereaved Parents and the Professional
When a Child in your School is Bereaved

Library of books on child bereavement

Cruse – Bereavement Care
(Bereavement counselling available throughout the UK)
126 Sheen Road
Richmond
Surrey TW9 1UR
Tel: (01) 940 4818
Registered charity no. 208078

Miscarriage Association
Secretary
18 Stoneybrook Close
West Bretton
Wakefield WF4 4TP
Tel: (0924) 830515

Stillbirth and Neonatal Death Society (SANDS)
28 Portland Place
London W1N 4DE
Tel: (01) 436 5881
Registered charity no. 299679

Leaflets:
The Loss of Your Baby at Birth or Shortly After (Stillbirth or
    Neonatal Death) available from Health Education Council
Notes on Initial Visit by a Befriending Parent
Guidelines for Bereavement Support Groups with Regard to
    Stillbirths and Neonatal Deaths

Ireland

Irish SIDS Association
13 Christchurch Place
Dublin 16

Scotland

Scottish Cot Death Trust
Royal Hospital for Sick Children
Yorkhill
Glasgow G3 8SJ
Tel: (041) 357 3946

International groups

Australia

National SIDS Council of Australia
(Also SIDS Research Foundation)
1227 Malvern Road
Malvern
Victoria 3144
Tel: 3 822 0766
Fax: 3 822 2995

Canada

Canadian Foundation for the Study of Infant Deaths
PO Box 190 Station R
Toronto
Ontario M4G 329
Tel: 416 488 3260
Fax: 416 483 4135

New Zealand

Dr Shirley Tonkin
National Children's Health Foundation
Cot Death Division
PO Box 28–177
Remuera
Auckland 5
Tel: Auckland 548 592

South Africa

Cot Death Society
c/o Mrs J Marais
PO Box 11306
Vlaeberg 8018

United States of America

National Sudden Infant Death Syndrome Clearing House
8201 Greensboro Drive
Suite 600
McLean
Virginia 22102
Tel: (703) 821 8955

National SIDS Alliance
330 N. Charles Street
Baltimore
Maryland 21201

National Sudden Infant Death Foundation
8200 Professional Place
Suite 104
Landover
Maryland 20785
Tel: (301) 459 3388
From outside Maryland (800) 221 SIDS

Addresses of European groups can be obtained from the
Foundation for the Study of Infant Deaths

Other organisations mentioned in this book

The Hon. Secretary
Coroner's Society of England and Wales
77 Fulham Palace Road
London W6 8JA

Tranx
17 Peel Road
Harrow
Middlesex HA3 7QZ

Release
1–4 Hatton Place
Hatton Gardens
London EC1N 8ND

Twins and Multiple Births Association (TAMBA)
Katy Gow
Chairwoman
1 Victoria Place
Kings Park
Stirling FK8 2QX

National Childbirth Trust (NCT)
Alexandra House
Oldham Terrace
London W3 6NH
Tel: (01) 992 8637

Foresight
The Old Vicarage
Church Lane
Witley
Surrey GU8 5PN

Index

Other titles in the **Survival Handbooks** series:

Shirley Cooklin
From Arrest to Release: The Inside/Outside Survival Guide

Sandra Horley
Love and Pain: A Survival Handbook for Women

Tony Lake and Fran Acheson
*Room to Listen, Room to Talk: A Beginner's Guide to Analysis,
Therapy and Counselling*

For further details, please write to the sales manager, Bedford
Square Press, London WC1B 3HU